Activism!

Direct Action, Hactivism and the Future of Society

TIM JORDAN

REAKTION BOOKS

Published by Reaktion Books Ltd
79 Farringdon Road
London EC1M 3JU, UK

www.reaktionbooks.co.uk

First published 2002

Series design by Libanus Press
Printed and bound by Biddles Ltd, Guildford and King's Lynn

British Library Cataloguing in Publishing Data
Jordan, Tim, 1959–
   Activism!: direct action, hactivism and the future of society – (FOCI)
   1. Globalization
   I. Title
   304.4'84

ISBN 1 86189 122 9

Contents

CHAPTER ONE

Societies in Pieces, Movements in Action

Past, Present, Future

As you wander down the aisles of supermarkets, half-concentrating, half-thinking of something else, it suddenly dawns on you that the shelf that you thought would be laden with bread is laden instead with various organic products. How did that happen? By now, the range of eggs on offer – organic, granary-fed, non-battery, battery – is no surprise, simply a part of a normal consumer day in an overdeveloped nation. Later the same morning, you are similarly half-concentrating while idly looking at job adverts, when the standardized claims of commitment to equal opportunities catches your eye. You suspect that this phrase would not have made sense to your grandparents. You realize that the future, which we normally expect to arrive grandly, also arrives in such small moments as these: changes in the appearance of supermarket shelves, the diversification in the production of eggs, the formalization of job-application procedures. With a final, idle thought, you even ask yourself 'How do new ways of living come into the world? How do we find new understandings of the right or good way to live?'

These are the questions that are explored in this book, which is about the ways in which 21st-century societies are generating meanings for 'the good life', and, as importantly, how such new meanings gain authority and come to affect our daily lives. The place where we will find answers to these questions is also familiar, though not so much a part of our daily lives as choosing eggs. This is problematic, because it is also too familiar, so its significance in creating the future is easily missed. Let us take a first look at it.

The scenes are familiar. Crowds of people are waving placards, chanting, taking over streets normally dominated by cars. The mass of wandering people are differentiated by banners, flags, sounds and dress. They are nearly always accompanied, if not surrounded, by police who march at the front and sides and can often be seen waiting, in groups, in side streets. If we cut to a related set of familiar images, we see a motley collection of young (mainly) men throwing bottles, hurling tear-gas canisters and yelling in a state of turmoil; they are confronted by black- and blue-uniformed, frequently armed police charging and retreating, carrying some of the motley crew off to waiting vans. There are other images that we have seen time and again: small boats with flags dodging around large tankers, great crowds of cross-dressing men and women celebrating their pride. Someone is dragged from up a tree or down a tunnel; someone knocks on a door and hands in a petition. All of these images represent political activism. These violent or peaceful, noisy or quiet actions taken by groups of people, some small and some huge, are attempts to alter society according to the desires of those taking action. These are some of the signs and moments of popular political activism, and they are integral to 21st-century societies.

These scenes are somehow too familiar. We know too well what is going on. Even when caught, by accident or design, within a protest, we hardly ever see it with inexperienced eyes. A group of people want change and are demanding action. Earth First!, for example, is an ecological activist organization that demands that the earth come first now! Political activists seek change to our societies *right away*: less pollution, more gun control, higher wages, less racial violence, less immigration, more public transport – a cacophony of demands. The real significance of activism rarely grips us; instead, the immediacy, drama and humour of protest cause us to focus on the meaning of particular movements and their demands. There is, of course, a more general question about the nature of popular political activism and our society. Both behind and as part of all of these familiar actions lies something unfamiliar and central to our futures, because it is within some of these movements that beliefs are being invented that may shape our future. From 'activism!' may come new definitions of the good life and society.

Certain types of political activism are creating new moralities which, when they gain the authority of mass acceptance, can inform changes in our societies. The future is given birth in the turmoil of people acting together politically. How can we understand all of the organic food in supermarkets and all those different types of eggs without reference to the modern 'green' or ecological movement? How can we trace the need for equal-opportunity regulations without connecting them to anti-racist and feminist ideas? The links between supermarket shelves and eco-activism or between feminism, anti-racism and job-application procedures need to be seen in their larger context; their place in our societies at large must be understood.

This book proposes to define this larger context in three unequal parts. In Chapter 2, different types of popular political activism are defined and the activism that is deriving new ethics for living is identified. The subsequent four chapters each examine a particular aspect of this activism: non-violent direct action and dis/organization, pleasure-politics, culture jamming and hacktivism. Each of these is a major theme that courses through 21st-century protests. In Chapter 7, these themes are drawn together to articulate the ethics that may underpin or inform future societies. We will meet all manner of actions, activists and ideas as we move through this story; in the end, we will see a vision that integrates the need to generate many different social solidarities and to contest many dissimilar social antagonisms in the context of radicalized forms of democracy. To set the scene for this exploration, this chapter will briefly outline political activism and its social context. This context will show that we can begin to see social movements as the source of authoritative ethical visions.

People Just Like Us

At a local school in London, in 1999, a new head teacher abolished the tradition of holding an Easter Bonnet Parade. In previous years, children had spent time making Easter-themed hats to wear in a parade. Some parents felt unhappy about this being cancelled, and when discussions about it broke down, they painted placards and held a small demonstration in the school yard. The funny Easter-hat parade had been replaced by collective action. In 1981, in Arizona, a group of people protested the building of the Glen Canyon Dam. While some distracted the police, others unrolled down the dam face a hundred-metre polythene strip with a crack printed on it, making the dam appear to be splintering. These are two examples of people acting together outside 'normal' institutional channels. Though different, they are both examples of collective action.

People take action together in many ways; entering a cinema when the doors open, or standing in a queue for a bus, are examples of collective action. What is under the microscope in this book is politically motivated collective action. At the outset, it is important to note that collective actions are numerous, often barely noticeable and, even when overtly political, taken by people just like us. Further, the word *politics* is an uncertain one nowadays, covering everything from the personal politics of conversation to the big boys' politics of national election campaigns. There are many different dimensions of the political, incorporating a wide range of human actions, feelings and social relations. To complicate matters even further, the familiar distinction of left, centre and right is also now problematic. A key example of this is the animal-liberation movement, which is hard to locate on the political spectrum of left to right because its ethical core involves denying any special right to the human species to kill or dominate other species. Where does the respect for non-humans fit into a political spectrum defined by the rights of humans? To gain a first view of political activism, we cannot look to definitional problems but should focus instead on collective actions that produce transgression and solidarity.

Transgression is essential to activism because collective action lacks a political aspect unless change is demanded. Whether that change is the end of global capitalism or the abolishing of an Easter-bonnet parade, the fact that some transgression of an existing state of affairs is called for is essential for a collective action to be political.

There are several ideas that need to be separated here. Transgression assumes that people live in ways they consider to be normal or unexceptional. People in the US and Europe generally expect to drive on the right-hand side of the road, whereas people in the UK and Australia do not. Certainly, people's 'normal' way of living changes over time, but at any one point certain conditions will be the 'usual' way. They may be so normal that people consider them to be natural. Transgression involves some change in these normal states of affairs. This change can be symbolic, for the normal conditions of life clearly involve many symbolic dimensions. When the Earth First! activists unfurled a giant, fake crack down the Glen Canyon Dam, they were transgressing the symbolic solidity of such a structure that is essential to its status as a normal part of life; a dam with a hundred-metre crack in it is simply not going to be accepted as routine. Attacks on or parodies of advertisements work in similar ways, transgressing the symbols that make up our daily lives. For example, in an advert that looks exactly like a Calvin Klein advert for the fragrance 'Obsession', a male model stares down into his stretched-out Calvin Klein underpants. In this instance, the culture jammers Adbusters are subverting both Klein and men's obsessions about their bodies.

Activism is essentially something done together by many people, but we must be careful with the sense of *group* or *collective* that is employed here. What is essential to activism is not simply being more than one, as we are in a cinema, but a sense of solidarity in pursuit of transgression. There has to be a sense of shared identity, which can best be understood at this stage as people recognizing in one another the anger, fear, hope or other emotions they feel about a transgression. Earth First! was formed in 1980 when five activists went out into the Mexican desert to discuss their common frustration with the American environmental movement's avoidance of radical transgresssion. The story goes that Dave Foreman called out 'Earth first' while Mike Roselle drew the clenched-fist logo under which all Earth First! organizations have campaigned since.[1] Another example comes from the women's anti-Cruise-missile protest camp at Greenham Common in the UK. One early participant recalled discussing the nature of the protest with an organizer: 'I wrote to Ann Pettitt and said, was it a feminist thing or was it a religious thing? And she rang me up and she said, no . . . No, it's people just like you.'[2] Thus each protest group initially formed as people recognized in each other frustrations, aspirations and desires to transgress the current state of the world. Solidarity is the result of such interactions, the recognition of a 'we' out of many separate 'I's.

Solidarity and transgression, collective and action, are the twins of activism. What separates activism from a crowd leaving a cinema, or groups gathered around listening to buskers, is that activists recognize in each other the desire to alter the usual ways their lives are lived. When leaving a cinema, all that most people want is to get outside in the same way they always do; the normal is desired, and any shift from it is likely to cause severe anxiety. The reverse is the case for activists, who desire, demand and work for change. Activism comes to life when people recognize in each other the will and desire to change the routines of life.

It complicates matters that such popular political action can no longer be grasped within the commonly understood politics of left and right. While it seems that choosing Earth First! and Greenham as examples of solidarity implies that activism is somehow normally a broadly left-wing position, this is not so. Earth First! USA has flirted with right-wing positions, such as the need to restrict immigration because it increases population pressures that are destroying the environment, and has long struggled with a split between near-eugenicist, patriotic defenders of the American wilderness and social-justice activists whose concerns include wider issues such as anti-racism and feminism (this latter wing became more influential in the 1990s and particularly so in Earth First! outside the US). Dave Foreman left Earth First! USA in 1990 calling for a 'group committed more to gila monsters and mountain lions than to people',[3] a position it is hard to imagine any left- or right-wing politician endorsing. We will explore in some detail what sorts of political values are being generated in activism and which sorts of activisms are creating new values, but it is important at the outset not to assume that current political activism is a covert continuation of politics defined by a right-to-left axis. Such an assumption misunderstands both the general nature of political activism and the nature of specific movements and organizations.

Activism conceived in this way is still very broadly defined (to be refined in the next chapter), but in the principles of transgression and solidarity we at least have a first definition. Before moving to a closer one, we can see how solidarities created to change what already exists can be set within the overall social conditions they affect and by which they are affected. We have seen an initial definition of activism, but we have not located it.

Twenty-first century Virtual, Network, Information, Complex, Global, Over-Developed Societies

Virginia Woolf famously claimed that human nature changed 'On or about December 1910'. Her description seems as apt for the beginning of the 21st century as she felt it to be for the beginning of the twentieth: 'All human relations shifted – those between masters and servants, husbands and wives, parents and children. And when human relations change there is at the same time a change in religion, conduct, politics and literature.'[4]

It is often now claimed that a new form of society emerged at the end of the twentieth century, one that can, perhaps, be dated to the fall of the Berlin Wall. Arguments continue, but it now seems that new social structures can be found in, among other things, changed family types, revolutionized communications, virtualized communities, globally organized production lines, branded consumption and re-ordered spiritual communities. The name of this new world is various, yet many argue that society is somehow different and that what it means to be human has (again) changed. For simplicity's sake, I will use perhaps the most common term for this changed world: the information society. To understand why popular political activism may be setting moral and ethical agendas, we can explore some central social institutions that have been transformed in the shift to information societies. We will see that part of each transformation dislocates a previously influential source of ethics, leaving the source of authority for ethical visions uncertain. What is important for activism is that in most dimensions of the information society, a disruption of the authority of pre-existing morality-defining institutions can be found. The key parts of the transition to the information society for activism and its ethical vision are those in which previously authoritative sources for ethics and morals have been dislocated. We can focus on a number of these in turn to see both the sorts of shifts typical of the emergence of the information society and where activism fits into these shifts.

Let us begin in the home, in the daily grind of who does the washing and cleaning and who controls the money. At one time, the answers to these questions might have divided clearly along gender lines. "'To be truthful," said Mrs Sanderson . . . "to be truthful, I don't know how much he earns, I only know what he gives me".'[5] Mrs Sanderson was a working-class wife in London in the 1950s; her words speak, at the everyday level, of a wider form of power: patriarchal power, the power of the father. This power was generally over members of the family, including younger males, but was, most importantly, of men over women. Children had marriages and employment to be defined, while spouses had their proper role and honour to be defended. Patriarchal power has been dislocated in the transition to information societies. The point is not that a feminist paradise has emerged, but that one way of authorizing the correct way to live is changing. Whether it results in a 'better' form of familial power is still open to question. To understand this, we can briefly examine an interlocking series of shifts in family patterns, in family and work and in sexualities.[6]

It is well known that family patterns have changed significantly. For example, rates of divorce rose throughout the latter part of the twentieth century, loosening a central bond in the foundation of patriarchal families. Increasing numbers of women are delaying child-bearing and managing careers. There is an increasing variety of family types, with numbers of single people, single-parent households and households containing children from several marriages or relationships all increasing. Control over reproduction has changed rapidly, with changes in contraception to help prevent pregnancy and changes in medical technologies to create pregnancy. Closely related to changes in family patterns are changes in patterns of work. Women have been entering employment in increasing numbers at the same time as many stable, working-class, classically male jobs have been migrating away from Western countries, often to 'developing' countries, where they are taken by much lower-paid women workers. These changes are caught up in wider globalizing trends within socio-economies, but they add up to increasing numbers of women working, particularly in part-time positions. This trend is fuelled by the lower pay that women have always received, and continue to receive, and because women may be more interested in flexible working patterns to help juggle child care and work responsibilities. At the same time, the assumption that heterosexuality is the normal or authorized form of sexuality has been challenged. This is important to patriarchal power because heterosexuality is a key component of the regulation of desire and reproduction of populations through which patriarchal governments exert power over the innermost components of people's lives. The latter can be seen in the emergence of non-heterosexual movements and communities, particularly in the emergence of families in which parents are not heterosexual.

Taken together, these three trends point to the father losing power he previously wielded, and this is true whether we are referring to the father of a family, the father of a nation or some other point of patriarchal power. This does not mean that some utopia has emerged. Some changes arguably produced worse lives. For example, women may find that they only have access to poorly-paid and part-time employment just as they are having to shoulder the dual burdens of being breadwinner and child-rearer. No assumption should be made that the undermining of patriarchal power leads automatically to a better world. At the same time, we can see one source of morality-giving fractured with the loss of patriarchal authority. The fact that this is a loss not just for many individual fathers, but for a whole range of patriarchal institutions that trade on the pre-eminence of 'father-figures' raises a second figure whose ability to define the good life and society has dissipated: the politician.

At the beginning of the 21st century, it might seem almost incomprehensible to claim that politicians once wielded moral authority. Financial, and other, scandals have touched many politicians, including the presidents and prime ministers of Germany, France, the US and the UK. The widespread realization that politicians vigorously manage the news, or, in current jargon, 'spin', means that it is hard to remember a time when it could be assumed that they were telling the truth. The problem here is not in arguing that politicians have little authority when defining ethical visions, but in remembering that this is a recent phenomenon. Part of the difficulty is that our current understanding has been projected back in history, allowing us to contemplate the priapism of John F. Kennedy, or to discuss whether the Japanese were deliberately allowed to bomb Pearl Harbor to ensure that the US entered World War Two. It seems, when we look back, that our current scandals have always been with us; after all, it is now widely accepted that whatever Churchill's achievements may have been, he was also drunk much of the time. But this is retrospective wisdom that fails to see that there were times when politicians articulated authoritative moral visions. It is true that politicians, because of the contested and representative nature of their profession, are possibly the least authoritative of the figures we are now examining, but this should not blind us to their loss of authority. There is a large gap between Franklin Roosevelt articulating the New Deal, or Churchill articulating a war effort, and John Major, when Prime Minister of the UK in the early 1990s, calling for a 'back-to-basics' morality campaign predicated on a non-existent England of cricket pitches and warm beer – or, for that matter, Al Gore and George W. Bush struggling to ensure that their partisan supporters decided the state ballot to put one of them in the White House.

A number of factors lie behind this shift. First, the cost of elections has risen, leading to the almost total dependence of democratic representatives on their financial backers. In systems where huge amounts of money are needed simply to have a fighting chance in an electoral contest, there is little possibility of candidates taking positions that will harm their backers. Second, major campaigns are now fought out almost entirely mediated by the media. Even if a candidate travels around meeting people, this tends to be in the service of images that will be shown through news broadcasts or print. However, the media are themselves driven by very different impera-tives than the presentation of complex policies or the exploration of detailed tax or spending plans. This has led to a politics of the sound-bite, with ever shorter amounts of time being given to political messages. So it may be understandable that politicians are often viewed as being in the pay of the rich and offering dishonest slogans rather than honest social policies because, at the beginning of the 21st century, that is what democratic systems demand of them. This convergence of finance and media is embodied by the once and future Prime Minister of Italy, Silvio Berlusconi, who was the head of Italy's largest private media corporation at the time he first became Prime Minister. That someone became the leader of a major Western nation who is not just dependent on both money from corpora-tions and time from the mass media, but simply *is* both these things, is almost by itself an explanation of why no-one trusts a politician.

The media not only participate in the de-legitimation of politicians, but have themselves sometimes been the source of moral authority. As with politicians, their ethical currency is currently so debased in many people's eyes that it is hard to remember when people trusted newspapers or television. However, at one time they did. In the US, the once-magister-ial figure of Walter Cronkite reading the evening news represented solidity and authority. Similar reassuring figures from the media could be found in many countries; they symbolized the authority of the media to present news and entertainment to their populations. In some countries, the pres-ence of a government-funded national broadcaster, such as the BBC in the UK or the ABC in Australia, represented the impartiality of the media. Faith in such media institutions has undergone a lessening similar to that experienced by authority figures.

There are a number of reasons for this. There has been a sudden profu-sion of different channels through which media can be presented. This is particularly true of television. While in the early 1970s there were often only three or four channels broadcasting to everyone in a nation, by the early 21st century there were hundreds of channels broadcasting in varying regional patterns. Access to these channels is often restricted by having to pay and to use particular forms of technology such as cable or satellite. At the same time that broadcasting has fragmented, ownership has been concentrated in the hands of a small number of media barons who control vast, world-wide holdings across different media; Berlusconi has been mentioned, but the small number of others includes Rupert Murdoch and Conrad Black. Media that are fragmented into narrowly targeted channels and are simultaneously owned by few people lose legitimacy, because they seem to serve only their narrowly defined audience and are subject to media masters adept at playing politics. In addition, the media's authority is undermined, because their tools have never been so accessible to individuals. It is now common for people to shoot their own videos, take pictures and, most importantly, distribute what they make. The production and distribution of images and text is easier than ever before. Technological changes are important here, with the Internet in particular providing an accessible means for people to both find and present their own information. The videotaping of the police beating of Rodney King that helped to ignite riots in Los Angeles in 1992 is an example of this grassroots access to media production. Between the fragmenting of media channels allied to concentration of ownership and the radical lowering of barriers to production and distribution of media, a powerful force has been created that reduces the authority of broadcast media. Walter Cronkite and his ilk now look like figures from history.

A final example of the decline in morality-giving authorities is the diminishing importance of institutionalized religions alongside the emergence of minority, new and fundamentalist forms of spirituality. Figures for an ongoing drop in the numbers of people attending church are commonplace when discussing 'crises of faith'. At the same time, figures for those attending or committed to splinter faiths or minority forms of spirituality are often thought to be rising. We can see, for example, the emergence of tele-evangelism in the US, where various mutant forms of fundamentalist Christianity have garnered large audiences and become associated with far right movements. In an opposite, yet corresponding, way, environmental movements have explored various pagan forms of spirituality including the use of sympathetic magic and the re-emergence of Druids. As many societies realize that they are multicultural, it no longer becomes a social goal to have one faith that unites a nation or region. For example, British schools are required to offer an act of worship, but this is not tied to any one religion, not even the establishment religion. As institutionalized forms of faith begin to lose their unquestioned right to be considered the 'majority', both because of declining numbers and because of the emergence of other forms of spirituality, the powerful figures of such religions begin to lose their moral authority. Perhaps no greater example of this lessening moral authority exists than the fact that, currently, a divorced adulterer (Prince Charles) is due to become the formal head of the Anglican Church when his mother dies, even though that Church holds marriage sacred.

This picture generally holds for Anglo-American or overdeveloped countries, but is not necessarily as accurate for other parts of the world. The continued power of Catholicism sometimes contrasts sharply with its weakening power on its home territory. However, some faith-lessening processes are visible across the world. For example, the emergence of Hindu nationalism in India both develops and confuses relations between social power and spirituality while challenging previously accepted understandings of spiritual authority. A final factor is the rise of various fundamentalist interpretations of religion, which tend to appeal to militant minorities while at the same time alienating majorities. Whether it is Islamic or Christian fundamentalism, both tend to undermine the faith of many in institutionalized religions while spawning outrages such as the 1995 Oklahoma City bombing and the World Trade Center atrocities. These, in turn, lead many individuals to despair even further of any spirituality. Again, a process can be seen of a once powerful moral authority not disappearing, but having to operate alongside other significant voices, thereby lessening its own pre-eminence.

Other possibilities could be explored. Statistics are widely held to be able to prove anything. Philosophers are considered irrelevant. Police are corrupt and admit, in some places, to institutional racism. Jobs are no longer for life. Musicians no longer strive for authenticity of feeling, but utilize machines to support manufactured groups who can themselves not sing properly. A cynical list could go on and on; it is the underlying point that needs to be made clear. Authority to offer visions of the good life, implying the ability to create moralities or ethics, has been displaced from many of its previous sources during the creation of the information society. Assuming that such displacements have occurred, we can ask whether anything has replaced these sources. Where do new ethical forms come from? Who got the free-range eggs into our shops?

Whose Pulpit?

One moment can symbolize the changes that I see occurring. On Easter Sunday 1998, Outrage! activists invaded the pulpit in Canterbury Cathedral during a sermon being delivered by the Archbishop of Canterbury, George Carey. Outrage! were protesting discrimination by the Church against lesbian and gay people. At one moment in the protest, leading Outrage! activist Peter Tatchell and leading Christian activist George Carey stood next to each other in the pulpit. This image prompts questions. Who is giving the lessons now? Who has the right to speak? Who is best using the pulpit to help us understand how to live? The answers may seem simple. Like all encounters with political activism, things are clear when a particular struggle is under the microscope; here was a conflict over the rights of different sexualities. Yet, as I have already said, it is not such specific politics that are important for my purposes, but the larger symbol. The pulpit is a key place and the Easter Sunday sermon a key time when Christianity calls attention to itself as the giver of norms, as an arbiter of how we should live. From the pulpit, the Church's official representative preaches values for life, something it has done for centuries. The Church is also perhaps the clearest example of a norm-giving institution, with its organizations and rituals calling on people to bow their heads before a Lord greater than any other. However, on 12 April 1998, a different normative call was made from the most powerful of the Anglican Church's public platforms, a call resting on an entirely different basis from the Church's divine legitimation.

Outrage! had been formed in the 1990s as the Aids crisis was devastating gay communities and gays were encountering few useful responses from established institutions, when they did not encounter outright contempt. Outrage! took direct action not just to try and force adequate healthcare for all of the population in relation to Aids and HIV, but also to attack prejudices against gays and lesbians that lay behind attitudes dismissing gay deaths as irrelevant or, worse, as righteous punishment. Outrage! activists for years placed their bodies and beliefs into spectacular events and grass-roots organizing to eliminate prejudice on the basis of sexuality and to allow the full possibilities created for all people by queer sexualities. To see Tatchell and Carey cheek-to-cheek in the pulpit offered a symbol of the passage from norm-giving institutions to ethical collective movements.

Perhaps in that moment we can see the role activism may be playing in our society. We can see a new way in which the beliefs, ethics and norms through which we understand the 'goodness', or otherwise, of our lives and societies are being generated. That moment is not about Carey and Tatchell as individuals, but as representatives of a shift from beliefs authorized by institutions, often rooted in the period of industrialization or earlier, to beliefs generated in the countless exchanges between activists in popular political movements floating in informational times. We need to be careful about this claim, though. It does not mean that activists are defining our future society; rather, they are part of the creation of values by which we may judge our future society. Activists are not inheriting the earth, they are not necessarily achieving their stated aims, but they are creating something both greater and lesser than their stated aims. They are offering new definitions of the good world. The list of such values that are now integral to our political, cultural and economic lives is long; feminism has fed into the post-1960s recreation of gender differences, Black liberation movements have formed ethics that underpin multicultural societies, the gay and lesbian movement has reconceived sex and the body, and eco-activists are making saving the planet common sense. Different movements are creating different ethical systems for information societies.

From many sources and in many ways, activism is generating the future of societies. This is not in the sense of planning a utopia, not in the sense of defining five-year plans whose fulfilment will lead to the new dawn, and not even in the sense of succeeding in immediate goals. Social movements, protest groups and activist networks are generating new ethical forms, new moralities, that are seeping into the smallest crevices of society and are becoming the ways in which we think the good life can be lived. Men and women should be equal, animals have a right to decent living conditions, the environment is essential to us all and is under threat, gun laws need to be tightened, fuel taxes are too high/low; all of these, and countless more claims from the left, right, centre and beyond of popular political activism, are beginning to coalesce into new definitions of a moral society. The remainder of this book will explore just how this is occurring and what morality is being brought into being.

CHAPTER TWO

Transgression: Reforming, Reactionary and Visionary

Transgression and Time

What has so far been called popular political activism is itself a varied field of collective actions. One symbol of this are the flags of the London eco-activist organization Reclaim the Streets!. They all have three colours – green for ecology, red for socialism and black for anarchism – but there is a range of different combinations and amounts. At a demonstration, you can take the flag whose blend best symbolizes your personal commitment. While socialism and, to an extent, anarchism are familiar in the context of left-to-right politics, ecology is not. It may have been associated with the left, but there is no necessary connection here. Ecology looks to the environment, a concern wider than the human interests that lie at the bottom of left-to-right politics. This, along with other examples already mentioned, such as the animal-liberation movement, means that we cannot begin by using the left-right axis to analyze popular political activism. Instead, we can take up a number of questions based on the sketch in Chapter 1 of activism, transgression and solidarity.

The use of the exclamation mark in 'activism!' will become important in these discussions. It follows, or is inspired by, the tendency of recent movements to exclaim about themselves: Earth First!, ActUp!. As this chapter progresses, we will gain a view of the historical context of all political activism and then categorize different types of present-day activism. Once this has been done, I will have defined the type of activism that might be producing ethics for a future society. It is this political activism that will then have the exclamation point added. This means that when I refer to activism, social movements, popular collective actions or some other of the many terms that are used to refer to our topic, I will be referring to all types of such political activity. But when I refer to activism!, I will be referring specifically to those movements that draw on the future to create the future. This method will cut through the occasional morass of terminology surrounding collective actions that can be called 'radical', 'alternative', 'popular', 'grass-roots', 'people-power' or simply 'social' (or 'cultural' or 'political' or 'economic') movements. One further scene-setting will be useful. We have already briefly placed activism in the context of the transition to information societies, but nothing has been said about its history. To ensure that the context for activism touches on all necessary points, it is important to include it.

The History of Activism

Popular or radical political activism has a long history. We need only think of those who claim that Jesus Christ was really a radical activist to see an ancient grass-roots organization aimed at social change. Instead of charting the history of activism from ancient times to now, however, it is more important to sketch in the relevant historical context for present-day activism. This means truncating history somewhat, but it also allows a focus that does not spread discussion too thinly. The key context for 21st-century political activism is the messy, uncertain and uneven transition from industrial to information society touched on in the previous chapter. I will focus on three stages of this transition while acknowledging that this is a broad sketch rather than an authoritative history. First, the emergence of industrial societies was accompanied by a range of social movements addressing a number of issues. The clearest examples are the labour movement, the Suffragettes' movement, the anti-slavery movement and movements both for democracy and against autocracy. Second, these swirling currents of political activism began to be channelled primarily through the political banks of class relations. The beginning of this process was marked by the Bolshevik Revolution. This does not mean that struggles became class, or Marxist, struggles, but that all struggles existed within a framework that saw class as the essential or fundamental political struggle. Third, by the 1960s, this channelling had begun to break down, and there was a re-emergence of many social movements, often called 'new social movements', that did not necessarily address class as the fundamental political category. These movements are familiar and include feminism, anti-racism and the ecological movement. A recasting of far-right movements such as those embodied by the British National Party, the National Front in France or the Northern League in Italy also occurred. We can look at these three historical moments in turn.

Political conflict at nearly all levels accompanied the emergence of industrial societies in the nineteenth century. International conflict occurred both in wars between sovereign states and in imperialist projects for subjugating other states. Cultural conflicts occurred over developments in representation, in communication media and over the definition of national cultures. Economic, social and other conflicts all intermingled as social structures were overturned and remade. As part of these changes, as both cause and effect, a number of social movements emerged out of popular political activisms. The Suffragettes struggled most famously over women's right to vote, but also touched on many different aspects of women's subjection to men, including contraception, marriage, the right to work and more. The anti-slavery movement gained pace throughout the century, achieving government support in Britain. Popular struggles over the nature of government continued throughout a period in which the widespread power of monarchy was seriously challenged and would eventually largely disappear in the morass of World War One. And everywhere, workers sought to form trade unions, to make bargains with employers and to legitimate their political rights, as well as improving their economic position. Though industrial society is sometimes reduced to its economic dimensions, it involved widespread changes in government, international relations and local and national cultures. Popular political activism in this time was part of, and reacted to, all of these types of changes, producing widespread activism on a wide range of issues. This diversity would become more channelled during the twentieth century.

The Russian Revolution was a key point in the twentieth century for political activism. It helped to establish the main political axis for popular political activism to be one based on class. It also helped to create a reinterpretation of the left/right political axis from its wider sense, created in the French Revolution, where forms of government were central to it, to a sense in which class relations were the fundamental political structure. This included the establishment of a strong relationship between nationalist and class politics, such that at times it has been difficult to separate nationalist from class politics. This development can roughly be seen in two stages, pre-Cold War and Cold War.

In the first stage, the example of the Russian Revolution seemed to offer many grass-roots campaigns an example of what could be achieved. It also, misleadingly, seemed both to confirm Marx's prediction of the end of capitalism and to be only the first in a series of European revolutions to come. Many commentators of the time felt the latter to be true. For example, the Bolshevik government, to its own peril, delayed signing a First World War peace agreement with Germany because it hoped that the

German proletariat would rise up and end the war through international revolution. The former notion was misleading, because though urban workers were important to the Bolshevik Revolution, Russia was a country only beginning the process of industrialization. If anything, the Bolshevik Revolution was a revolution in contradiction to Marx's predictions that upheaval would come in the most developed capitalist economies.

Though both of these ideas can, with hindsight, be seen to have been false, at the time it was not so easy. The various insurrections in Germany and what can be called the near-revolution there after the end of World War One, then the Great Depression and the General Strike in Britain, along with other class-based conflicts, all seemed to point to class and labour politics being the central political divide, with Russia always looming in the background as the possible future. This is not to say that all political struggles of this time were defined around class interests; to claim this would be, for example, to ignore anti-colonial campaigns such as that in India. What can be seen emerging, however uncertainly and amid many different struggles, is a framework that saw the fundamental political struggle to be class-based. This meant that all struggles did not have to be centred on class, but all had to define themselves in relation to class politics.

With the emergence of the Cold War, the sense that the world was divided into two warring political, cultural and economic camps was sustained by powerful institutional forces. These forces were greatly strengthened by the Chinese Revolution and other post-war transformations, such as those in Cuba or Vietnam. These two camps saw their key dividing lines to be around issues of class – communism versus capitalism – and this finally established class as the fundamental divide for political activists. Again, it did not mean that other types of political struggle – democracy, nationalism, human rights, ethnicity and more – disappeared, but that they were all operating in a political field constituted by class politics. This meant that, without giving up their particular goals, each struggle had to position itself in relation to class and the Cold War, whether it did so by rejecting class and struggling for some different political goal or by integrating class conflict within its movement.

The effects of this framework can be seen in various areas, one being anti-colonial struggles. Here, post-war, a number of colonized nations sought their independence by employing a range of political interests such as the nation, ethnicity and legal rights rather than just class interests. But in nearly all cases, anti-colonial struggles had to work out their relationships to both class and Cold War actors. For example, in the Cuban revolution, many see, rightly, an uprising with important national dimensions. This is, at least in principle, in contradiction to the revolution's proclaimed socialism, which was internationalist. Even at the price of such contradictions, the nationalist and peasant interests underpinning the Cuban revolution had to be related to class. Similarly, the work of Frantz Fanon analyzes colonialism and the struggle against it at many levels – the psychology of racism, nationalism, democracy – but as his work developed, he placed these in relation to the class basis of colonialism. This is not meant to deny or subject all of his work to one political principle; instead, it illustrates how class was the factor that entered all political discussions. It also illustrates that the framework for political resistance after the Second World War contained one inescapable political problem, among many others: the labour/capital divide.

Even as class moved to centre-stage, in the wings, other struggles were maintaining themselves and becoming more certain of their goals. These stirrings can be found not only in anti-colonial struggles, where issues of nation and race could never be finally absorbed into class politics, but also in struggles among peasant and indigenous communities over land and civil rights. The latter began to frame a non-class politics, particularly in the American civil-rights movement, but also in the civil-rights struggle in Northern Ireland. However, in the context of upheavals in overdeveloped countries, particularly the US over the Vietnam War, the 1960s also saw a flowering of radical class struggles. With such spectacular points as the

May 1968 uprising in France, where student occupations were accompanied by a near-general strike, many felt that the prophecy of revolution might finally (again) be drawing near. Many student societies strengthened Marxist interpretations of both the world and political strategy. Most notably, the extraordinary creativity of the May events in France led to hyper-Marxist, often Maoist, political groups who continued what they saw as the path to revolution while, at the same time, becoming ever more estranged from working-class organizations. All through these times, other movements were emerging and growing in strength, often in opposition to revolutionary class-based groups. For example, and perhaps most famously, one cause of the second-wave feminist movement was the failure of radical student movements to offer women a significant role. The now-famous occasion when a prominent student-militant described the role of women in the movement as 'prone' (meaning on their backs and available to male militants for sex) is an emblem of such contradictions and interactions between radical groups. Black-power groups and post-civil-rights-movement groups began to reflect on a political vision primarily based on racial oppression rather than one necessarily integrated with class politics. In the early 1970s, gay and lesbian struggles emerged both in their own right and from within some of these new movements, for example through the place of lesbians within second-wave feminism.

One of the things these struggles shared was a renewed focus on their particular struggle as the primary repression. This implicitly rejected class as the primary or master oppression to which all struggles had to relate. This does not mean that class was absent from these new social movements – far from it – but it does mean that from early in their lives these movements had a critical attitude to class. Most such movements have spent a long time since the 1970s trying to work out their relations to class movements and struggling over the place of class oppression in relation to gender, racial, sexual or other oppression. What now seems reasonably clear is that from the 1970s on, popular political activism began to shift from a general framework that saw class as the primary political determinant to one that acknowledged many different political struggles as of equal importance. Such a shift did not rule out class conflict, but moved it from being the struggle that all other struggles had to position themselves against to being one struggle among many.

By the 1990s, the hierarchy of oppressions had been broken. No one activist struggle could, in a general sense and with any authority, establish itself as more fundamental or important than any other. While activists from within struggles often feel themselves to be engaged in *the* struggle, the more general direction of popular activism can now be seen in over 30 years of post-1960s activism, and it is towards many different struggles, none of which is assumed to be more fundamental, more encompassing or more significant than others. This multiple context for transgression in political activism needs to be kept in mind, as it dislocates us from many habitual political principles. In particular, the political axis of left to right needs to be handled carefully, as it has, so often, been a proxy for labour-to-capital political interests. Though the latter are clearly still important, they can no longer be assumed to encompass or underpin popular activism.

The key consequence of this argument is that we need to understand which popular activisms draw on the future. Using the terminology introduced earlier, we need to separate activism! from activism within the historical context just outlined. Additionally, we need to see how to understand different types of activist movements. To determine this, let us look in more detail at the issue of transgression.

Snowdrop and Transgression

Transgression is an assault on the way social norms, beliefs, inequalities and oppressions are reproduced. The opposite to transgressive social change is political action to generate a different world that is, simultaneously, a confirmation of the existing one. In other words, any change also reaffirms that society goes on as before. Changes in the law, however radical, reaffirm the process of legal change itself and legitimate the institutions of representative government that produce it. In contrast, transgression may produce a different world, creating new ways of making change. Revolutionary movements seek not new legislation, but new forms of democracy and new ways of making laws. This is an analytical distinction, of course; movements often embody both of these types of social change or some point between them. For example, feminism seeks both a radical destruction of patriarchy and legislation mandating equal pay. Though these two types of political action are often intertwined and can be difficult to distinguish, they are distinct and, through their opposition, give us a point from which we can begin to define transgression. Let us now look at a movement that embodied one of these two ends of popular political action: the Snowdrop Campaign. This will make it possible to define transgression more clearly.

There are many popular campaigns that call for social change but which cannot be termed transgressive. Their social conservatism is masked by their commitment to change, often pursued with passion and mass action, but in fact they enhance the authority of existing social institutions, such as governments, courts, laws or appeals bodies, by appealing to their judgement. Many campaigns begin with this political world-view and never feel any need to question or move beyond it. In France, for example, farmers' protests are often violent and spectacular, but are also often aimed at forcing the government to change policies rather than forcing the nature of the government to change. In campaigns such as these, we find many of the symbols of popular protest – street demonstrations, petitions, spectacular media events – but all in the service of pressure on those in power, not in the cause of a redefinition or explosion of power.

The Snowdrop Campaign for gun-law change exemplifies this combination of change and non-change. In 1996, a man entered a school in

Dunblane, Scotland, and shot dead sixteen young children and their teacher. It was a horrific, extraordinary and devastating event. In its wake came a desire to prevent any repetition. A campaign emerged to reform legislation on the availability of hand-guns. Britain, like most countries, does not grant it citizens a constitutional right to bear arms; the power to restrict the availability of guns rests clearly with the national government, which can make any determination it wishes in this area. A campaign of popular protest was begun, focused on legislative change to restrict the availability of hand-guns. It was called the Snowdrop Campaign.

Snowdrop took up many of the 'normal' means of producing social change, such as lobbying members of political parties or seeking media attention, as well as some of the more 'radical' avenues, such as street protests. The power and popular support for this campaign was considerable, as was demonstrated by its petition gaining over a million signatures. Pressure from Snowdrop was strong enough that the traditionally gun-supporting British centre-right party passed a partial ban on hand-guns (large calibre only). Soon after this, a change of government saw the British centre-left party in power, and it extended the ban to small-calibre hand-guns. Not all agreed with Snowdrop, but its opponents' arguments often seemed ineffective, if not trivial, compared to the Dunblane massacre. For example, some claimed that a ban on small-calibre handguns would ruin Manchester's chance of hosting the Commonwealth or Olympic Games, because the sport of shooting would be illegal. The loss of a sporting contest, however internationally significant, was hardly an effective riposte to the loss of seventeen lives.

The Snowdrop Campaign achieved its self-determined ends, something that many popular protests would find it difficult to claim. These ends existed entirely within the social system of the UK, posing no threat at an economic, cultural or political level. Social change occurred, guns were banned, but social change also did not occur, in the sense that the representative government controlled and determined change. The responsiveness of the system demonstrated its legitimacy, which ultimately rested on broad support for the change enacted. For example, gun control has an entirely different meaning in the US. There, the fact that, for example, one in four Americans have been threatened with a gun has not led to broad support for restricting access to guns; instead, it has led to many people concluding that they need a gun as well. When Snowdrop campaigners spoke at a pro-gun-control rally in the US, there was a counter-demonstration by Armed Informed Mothers. Even such compromise measures as child-proof trigger locks on guns were opposed. A spokeswomen from Armed Informed Mothers had defended herself with a gun against an attack by her violent ex-husband and told the media 'Thank God, my firearm was unencumbered by a trigger lock.'[1] We see in this contrast between the US and the UK how closely associated some popular campaigns are with legitimate social institutions. Change on guns in the UK was possible because the government felt that broad support for gun-control existed. Where this support does not exist, campaigns relying on existing social institutions tend to fail.

To generalize this point: the success or failure of campaigns like Snowdrop is defined from within the same system that allows the identification of the object of the campaign. The demand for change and the means of change exist within one coherent social and institutional framework. If we articulate this in terms of time, we can say that Snowdrop relied on the present and, in doing so, reinforced the institutions of the present. A similar example is the rejection by most trade unions of radical demands for the overthrow of capitalism in favour of struggles for better wages and conditions, these being pursued through known and, usually, agreed avenues. For unions, the mechanisms can vary from factory-based committees to nationally, or even internationally, agreed wage and career structures, but they seek to resolve an ongoing process of social change through agreed mechanisms. By definition, nothing fundamentally new can come from such processes, whatever good they may do. The desires of these popular movements are formed within the same logics as the cultural, economic or political systems that create the desire for change in the first place. They represent the fine-tuning of social systems, not their reconstruction, and in this sense always represent the present.

Transgression and Zapatismo

At the other end of the continuum to campaigns such as Snowdrop are transgressive movements, movements that seek social changes that redefine social structures. These campaigns reject existing institutions, sometimes envisaging new ones as well as processes that are completely different to those that already exist. Or, more simply, such campaigns make demands that cannot be met within existing structures. For example, some radical feminist demands that men and women create separate communities until men give up patriarchal habits cannot be accommodated within many current societies' patriarchal structures. Radical environmentalists may demand that global socio-economies move completely to renewable energy sources, that people's consumption cultures shift from 'throwaway' habits to recycling, and that living standards in the overdeveloped world drop, both to allow equalization all over the globe and to protect the environment; it is almost impossible to see how such a list of demands could be accommodated within existing social structures. The list of radical initiatives could go on. We could look back in history to the Bolshevik Revolution and see in it the almost total transformation of such basic social facts as private property and employment. In each case, what we find is a refusal to stay within known rules of the political game. This attitude can be played out in tactical as well as ethical dimensions. For example, it has become commonplace for groups planning public demonstrations to agree a route and timing with the police. Marches can then be carried off peacefully and within police definitions of public order.

However, some groups have little interest in allowing the police to define what public order might or might not be. Such groups define demonstrations that are, as much as possible, kept secret from the police and around which police have to improvise. Even at the level of a single event, there are distinctions in activist groups between reinforcing existing social institutions and transgressing them.

So transgression, in the context of current popular political activism, is the contradiction of existing social structures, institutions and ethics. The ethics of the future can only come from transgression, from reaching beyond current ways of negotiating social conflict and resolving differences. The opposite end to transgression, on the continuum of political activism, always reinforces what exists; it reforms, but it does not change. Transgression reaches out for a different future; reforming moulds the future to the present.

There is one common misunderstanding of this interpretation of transgression. It is not the case that a transgressive movement or campaign must aim at all social institutions and structures simultaneously. Rather, transgression comes from the identification of problems with at least one social institution or structure of such magnitude that they cannot be solved from within that institution or structure. The fluidity of popular political activism is such that within and between movements, different social institutions can be identified as a component of society that needs changing. Different movements or parts of movements will identify and attack different parts of society, even conceiving society in entirely dissimilar ways to each other or in different ways within a movement. For example, the Zapatista movement in the Chiapas region of Mexico combines a basis in indigenous people's rights with an attack on 'neo-liberalism'. The former notion includes demands that indigenous peoples have rights to control their own lands and communities and they be recognized as full Mexican citizens. The Zapatistas understand the latter notion as a political ideology and programme lying behind a form of globalization that serves powerful economic interests, helping to exploit the poor. The movement's political analysis and identification of enemies flows around these two ideas.

Two sets of political change come from these political ethics, and each identifies different political paths. Here is how the Zapatista support group, ActLab from Texas, characterize Zapatista politics:

They [the Zapatistas] are against 'neoliberal' economic policies which include such things as: privatizing state systems of production (oil, transportation, etc.), removing subsidies and tariffs which protect small farmers, and using a "less government" rationale for providing less health and educational assistance to impoverished people. They [the Zapatistas] would like indigenous people to be decently paid for the work they do, have arable land to farm (instead of the rocky cliffsides they work now), and have access to health and educational facilities.[2]

The social changes needed to enact these two sets of demands are, formally at least, very different. The latter set of demands – decent pay for work, access to arable land, access to health and education – could be met, in theory, by any representative government within many forms of capitalism. In fact, within Mexico these demands are more radical than they may seem, as they uncover generations of suppression and exploitation of indigenous peoples. Yet they do not formally contradict even Mexico's existing systems of representative government.[3] However, the first set of demands noted by Actlab could not formally be met because they identify neo-liberal policies that underpin economic forms of globalization demanded by both Mexican capitalists and the overdeveloped nations. To enact Zapatista demands here would amount to Mexico revolutionizing its relationship to capitalism and placing itself far closer to Cuba than to the US. This example shows how even in one movement, different demands and understandings of oppression can lead to different conceptions of what is and is not transgressive.

Across the range of social movements that exist within the modern world, there is no one structure or system that can be transgressed. Rather, there are many different systems conceived on the basis of the ethics and activism of each movement. This does not mean that movements cannot exchange ideas and move towards one another. The Zapatista attack on neo-liberalism has had wide resonance and been part of a shift within some green movements to participation in anti-neo-liberal globalization protests. Yet it remains the case that what might be transgressive for one movement, may not be for another. The social system or institution that must be made anew for one movement may be a vehicle for change for others. For example, some argue that legal systems must be transgressed because they presume private property as a given, and private property is inherently exploitative. In contrast, there are groups for whom legal changes recognizing their right to exist might be transgressive, for instance in religious groups or movements based on sexual preference.

Transgression is only apparent when there is an attempt to turn at least some part of the world upside down. Transgressive movements may also operate on two registers. At one level, they may demand changes from existing social institutions and thereby accept, in some sense, the legitimacy of those institutions, while at another level, they may seek the entire reconstruction of social systems. Transgression in this complex and multiple way separates activism from activism!. Transgression helps to distinguish movements that make the future in the image of the present from movements that create visions of a different future. Activism! must be transgressive, whereas activism can operate as Snowdrop does and change society while also conserving it.

But transgression is not enough to separate activism! from activism. There are also issues of time to consider.

Past, Present and Future

> For some strange reason, the Zapatistas speak to the future. I mean our words don't fit in the present, but are made to fit into a puzzle that is yet to be finished.
>
> Subcomandante Marcos[4]

Having articulated one relationship between time and activism, we can posit a second one to distinguish movements that may be creating norms on the basis of which our futures might be constructed. This process can be based directly on the relationship between time and transgression. As we have seen, movements that work within social systems exist in the present. From this use of the present, we can distinguish transgressive movements that look to the past or the future to criticize the present. For some, the present is a prison, caging all into a worse life than is necessary or decent. Such criticisms must come from somewhere; there must be a basis on which claims can rest that the present is unjust. That basis cannot be the present, because to work from the values of the present is to work from within your prison.

Two distinct types of popular protest emerge when activism becomes radicalized, when it is transgressive. Activists who believe that the present is no longer enough can look to the past. One politics creates a past in which life was superior to current times. History is pressed into service for visions that point us to a better society. A second politics looks to the future and the unknown. This is where we find activism!.

In a strict sense, movements that aim to create the future by going back in time re-act. Thus it is no surprise that most such movements are reactionary and at least flirt with authoritarianism. This does not mean that they are backward; they can often be as advanced in their use of technology or forms of organization, for instance, as any other movement. One example of such a movement is the Patriot movement in the US, which draws its values from America's foundation more than two hundred years ago. This past provides fertile ground in that it validates such rights as that to bear arms or to form militias, on the basis of which the wrongs of the present can be identified and popular mobilizations begun. William Peirce, the editor of the *National Vanguard*, has expressed a key analysis of the Patriot movement succinctly:

> . . . for the initiated, the New World Order . . . is a utopian system in which the U.S. economy (along with the economy of every other nation) will be 'globalized'; the wage levels of U.S. and European workers will be brought down to those of workers in the Third World; national boundaries will for all practical purposes cease to exist; an increased flow of Third World immigrants into the United States and Europe will have produced a non-White majority everywhere in the formerly White areas of the world; an elite consisting of international financiers, the masters of the mass media, and managers of multinational corporations will call the shots; and United Nations 'peace keeping' forces will be used to keep anyone from opting out of the system.[5]

Peirce's magazine bases itself on these insights, extending them particularly into anti-Semitic and racist views. While the entire Patriot movement cannot be identified with Peirce's views – like all modern social movements, it is a varied, networked collection of organizations, individuals and ideas – he puts his finger on one of the core analyzes driving it: the gradual takeover of the world and domination of the US by international bodies. For example, in May 1996 there was a ceremony at Holloman Air Force Base in the state of New Mexico at which German jets flew, the German Defence Minister was the host, and the German flag was displayed above the American one. The ceremony marked the opening of a training base for German pilots. Many saw this as yet another step on the road to

Peirce's New World Order. A Pentagon spokesperson was forced to issue an official denial that this was a German base or that American sovereignty had been infringed, stating: 'I would describe it not as a base; they are tenants.'[6] Examples like this are found across the Patriot movement, with certain issues providing an ongoing focus. In particular, any attempt at arms control is understood as another step in disarming the American population to control it. An analysis of reasons for disarmament published within Patriot groups that claims to be based on government documents argues:

> Both of these [government] booklets explain how our military is to be reduced to 2.1 million men. China and the Soviets are to be reduced to that level also. At this point, we are at Stage I at which time we are to transfer (on a permanent basis) one-half of our armed forces to be merged with the Russian and Chinese armies. In Stage II, the remaining one-half of our armed forces is then turned over to this same Security Council of the United Nations. The person in charge of the merged armies must, by agreement, always be a Russian. The world's smaller nations turn 100% of their armies over to the same undersecretary of the Security Council in Stage II.[7]

This excerpt was published in the Militia of Montana newsletter 'Taking Aim', but the same analysis has appeared a number of times within Patriot circles. 'Taking Aim' opens with the declaration 'ONE BULLET AT A TIME: THAT'S HOW YOU'LL GET OUR GUNS' and includes a heartfelt letter pleading with 'Peace Officers' not to force a militia member to shoot them. The right to carry guns points us to the Patriot movement's relationship to the past, as they justify and defend their right to bear arms as a right created when America was founded.

The Patriot movement, though it embraces modern technologies such

as the Internet, looks resolutely to the American Revolution and its after-
math for values. However futuristic the vision of the New World Order may
seem, the values that oppose it and on which the Patriot movement is
based derive from the past. One of the many examples of this can again be
found in the Militia of Montana's document explaining what the militia is.
In this piece, there does not appear to be any gap between the founding of
America and the present day, and the 'founding forefathers of this great
country' are quoted as the authorities for the legitimacy of modern-day
militias:

> Our forefathers knew that countries with a militia excelled, and
> nations without a militia usually failed. They knew that without
> certain safeguards inserted in our constitution, this nation would
> also fail . . . Keep in mind what the Militia is for, as Thomas
> Jefferson said: '. . . as a last resort, to protect themselves against
> tyranny in government.' . . . Jefferson couldn't have been more
> right! We are slowly loosing our sovereignty and being consoli-
> dated under one rule, and that one rule will eventually do away
> with the Constitution and rule with an iron fist.[8]

Harking back to the foundation of America also has a broader function. Not only is the Constitutional right to bear arms constantly quoted in
Militia documents, but their general ethic refers back to a mythical time of
small-town communities, freeing themselves from the yoke of an imper-
sonal, imperial government. It may strike some as ironic that within the
collective imagination of the Patriot movement the American government
assumes the place of the British colonial oppressor, but this is an accurate
representation of how the movement conceives itself and its enemy. This
ideal of small-community based freedom is also often, though not always,
used to justify attacks on feminists for undermining the traditional family,
on Jews for controlling and developing the New World Order and on non-

Whites for supporting a government that pays them off in welfare. The Patriot movement is undoubtedly connected to and constituted by many far-right ideas and organizations. It is also active and widespread. It was the Oklahoma Bomber, Timothy McVeigh, who wrote to a newspaper some time before he detonated the bomb that cost 168 lives: 'America is in serious decline. We have no proverbial tea to dump . . . Do we have to shed blood to reform the current system?'[9] McVeigh's connection of the American Revolution to the decline of America at the end of the twentieth century is emblematic both of the source of the Patriot movement's social vision and of the potential seriousness of the movement's actions.

For our purposes, it is the movement's attitude to time that is key. Here, we see a movement engaged with what it believes is a fundamental problem of the most futuristic, even science-fictional, kind: the suppression of liberty world-wide by an international government through the disarmament of the citizens of the United States. But however firmly the Patriot movement has its eyes fixed on change, however strongly it focuses on what the US will be like in ten or more years, the movement's vision of a better future comes from the past. The past both offers a basis for visions of the good society, and limits these visions to what can be authoritatively 'found' in the past.

A past of such fantasy that there is no reasonable basis to believe it once 'really existed' would have little authority. For example, a movement that took Tolkien's Middle Earth as real would have difficulty convincing people that it offered a historical basis upon which social values could be founded. However much people might enjoy, even become committed to, the ethics of Tolkien or others like him, they do not create credible bases for collectively imagined social change.

This comparison to 'clearly' fictional worlds allows us to clarify the historical 'reality' on which reactionary movements base themselves. This reality cannot be 'what really happened' in the past. There is no direct access to the past; it has gone forever. Instead, there are histories or, in these cases, usually reconstructions of the past based on various sorts of evidence: official documents, pictures, paintings, diaries, even reconstructions and role-playing. What reactionary movements both rely on and are restrained by is the construction of a plausible past on the basis of some body of evidence. Of course, such evidence will be selected partially according to the existing prejudices or beliefs of whoever is constructing the history, though each reconstruction will usually be presented as objective and morally neutral. Of course, history is no more value-free than science or sociology. Such processes must nonetheless be gone through for a reactionary movement to know what its beliefs are, for it to grasp the society it lost and seeks to recreate. Reactionary movements are constrained by the past in the sense that they are constrained to create an authoritative evidence-based vision of it. Rather than generating new values, they mine history for something they believe they have lost.

The past inspires but also incarcerates, because for it to be a solid political foundation it must be plausible. Entirely new ethics or values cannot be found here; by definition they cannot be generated from the past, as they cannot be new if it is credible that they already exist. This is not to deny that the past can be used differently by different people. There is no doubt that many opposed to the Patriot movement also invoke the American Revolution to justify their politics. Even given the important qualification that the past does not provide ready-made answers for the present but must be mined for relevant ideas, it remains true that searching the past results in the discovery of the old, not the new. This search should not, however, be thought of as a cynical process, as is sometimes claimed, a process by which people justify their politics through a selective and blinkered appropriation of evidence. Rather, the past really exists for such activists in that it provides inspiration for a better world. History, of a type, is really utilized, and here lies both the strength and the limitation of this kind of radicalism. The websites and publications of the Patriot movement contain not just speculative conspiracy theories but minutely researched historical articles. These may undoubtedly be questioned, but there is no denying the seriousness with which this movement, and reactionary movements in general, regard the foundation of their vision in past worlds.

Visionary Indigenese

Reactionaries oppose the past to the present in order to mould the future. Reformers pit the present against the present in order to shape the future. Transgressive movements that base themselves on the future to mould the future have a different source for ethics or social visions. The future is unknown; unlike the past, it does not provide ready-made myths, symbols and monuments waiting to be articulated into politics. For movements based on the future, it will be neither a recaptured past nor an updated present but a new kind of life unknowable in the present. Such a perspective poses undoubted problems, as it seems to offer a politics dedicated to the unknowable. Activist!s in these movements have to resolve a radical indeterminacy. A useful first example are indigenous people's rights movements like the already mentioned Zapatistas or the Amerindian movements, which are trying to generate a place for themselves in societies that only came into existence over their dead bodies.

It might be expected that such movements would look firmly back to a past when their customs and cultures, or their control of land, was undisputed. Many indigenous people's movements are rightly focused on the deep and irreparable damage that has been done to their communities. For example, if we look at the Australian Aboriginal community, we see that nations and cultures that had developed for tens of thousands of years were subject to explicitly genocidal policies, some of which continued as late as the 1970s. Despite the relative wealth of Australia, Aboriginal people are consistently measured as having levels of poverty and ill health as high as can be found anywhere in the world. Aboriginal activists have set against their dire colonial history and awful post-colonial present a range of demands including fundamental claims, such as control over land, and reforming demands, such as better access to healthcare or work. During the two-hundredth anniversary of the colonization of Australia, Aboriginal activists reminded all Australians of their long pre-colonization history and the fact that they had never, unlike the Maori people of New Zealand, negotiated or signed a treaty ceding control of their country. In satirical comment on these facts, one Aboriginal elder travelled to England and, standing on the cliffs at Dover, claimed England for the Aboriginal nation.

This might seem to draw Aboriginal activism towards the past, yet when examined closely, such politics seem as much, if not more, dependent on the future. The goal of most Aboriginal activism does not seem to be a return to old times, when they travelled Australia meeting only other Aboriginal nations and cultures. Whether happily or not, it is recognized that the past has gone. Non-Aboriginal Australians, who come from all over the world, will not be returning to their original national homes even if such homes could be defined. Rather, Aboriginal activists seek a complicated and so far nonexistent settlement that will allow them to take forward their cultures and civilizations, bringing their history with them into a more just post-colonial, multicultural Australia, not a pre-colonization Australia.

The example of land rights is important here, not only because it is a transgressive demand whose pursuit has altered the entire legal basis on which Australia rests, but because it attempts to re-articulate the Aboriginal relationship to land and community in a way that both meets Aboriginal needs and takes colonization into account. Under some limited circumstances, Aboriginal communities may claim legal title for lands. The process that occurs during a land-rights claim is that Aboriginal people must prove a continual and ongoing relationship to the land they are claiming (only certain types of government-owned land can be subject to such claims). This proof can be created in a number of ways. For example, farm records can be examined to create genealogies to prove that living Aboriginal people are direct descendents of individuals who lived on farms when they were first created. Elements of Aboriginal cultures, such as stories, dreamings, sacred objects or sites, can be shown to an investigating tribunal in an attempt to translate Aboriginal cultures and conceptions of land into ones that can be understood and adjudicated by Australian courts. This complex cultural translation can best be captured by noting that though the language of land-rights claims is a Western one of private property ('Do the Aboriginal communities own the land?'), Aboriginal communities often articulate this question differently, saying not that the land belongs to them but that they belong to it. While land-rights demands have only been met, at best, partially, and a centre-right government during the 1990s did what it could to destroy the limited rights that already existed, the desires articulated by Aboriginal people look to an unknown future. These demands, and even their partial satisfaction, not only change the status of Aboriginal people, but also that of any Australian citizen, by recognizing that some citizens have particular rights because of the invasion and colonization of Australia. In the course of these changes, the legal doctrine legitimating the European invasion of Australia – *terra nullius*, which declared the land legally empty when Europeans arrived – was overturned. What it means to be Australian and what Australia means have been reconfigured in this struggle.

Another campaign is relevant here. During the 1990s, Aboriginal activists began to call for an apology from their invaders for the long-lasting and brutal policy of taking Aboriginal children away from their parents and raising them elsewhere. This policy, which ended in the 1970s, was designed to hasten the demise of Aboriginal peoples by dispersing them within the wider community. As part of the campaign, 'sorry books' were opened throughout Australia in which anyone could add their personal apology – millions did so. Many government officials, as well as major cultural figures, participated, though the then Prime Minister refused to do so. Again, this may seem like a politics rooted in the past, its focus being a government policy that had ended but whose effects were ongoing. Yet we can see that this campaign existed only because of a future in which a nation split between its indigenous and its colonial peoples could only change once the two had acknowledged their past relationships and made amends. Thus it is the future that draws protest forward, not the past that calls it back.

Aboriginal activists are focused, with great passion and creativity, on the future of Australia and work to ensure that this future will include an ethical and just relationship between indigenous and non-indigenous Australians. Similar demands are heard from the Zapatistas, who often use the Mexican flag to symbolize both their exclusion from the nation and their desire to create a settlement that will make Mexico's indigenous peoples also Mexican; as they put it, 'Never again a Mexico without us.' What might seem to be some of the clearest examples of activism focused on the past turn out to be visionary activism!s attempting to draw on a future to change the present.

We have developed a distinction among transgressive activists between those who pit the past against the present and those who pit the future against the present. In both cases, it is the future that is at stake; it is social change that is sought. But only one movement draws clearly from new ground. Reinterpretations of the past will always be at least partially subject to their history, to what the past can legitimately support. Reactionary movements tend to know exactly what they want because they rely on their sense of loss. Visionary movements can be far more uncertain, because they place a radical indeterminacy at the heart of their ethics, but they also determinedly drive towards the future. Such movements do not judge the present world against a blueprint for utopia but against a belief that the world can be different, radically different, and that they are travelling towards just such a future.

Left, Right and Centre or Reforming, Reactionary and Visionary

No social movement is unified around one core vision; all circulate constantly around different ideas. Not all components of a social movement are drawn together with a common organization, membership and ideas. The type of unified organizational structure that sometimes emerges from working-class movements, for example, in the hierarchical world of formalized trade unions or the democratic centralist world of Marxist-Leninists, is not applicable to the vast majority of social movements. Transgressive activists at work in the 21st century may form organizations, but they are never subject to one organization. Thus while we explore movements based on the future, we will constantly touch upon other movements because of their networked or dis/organised nature.

It should be reiterated that while we have examined movements that might be placed on the dominant political axis of industrial society – left, centre and right – we have now identified a different axis that cuts across and confuses such an approach. It might seem obvious that the Patriot movement is a far-right movement and Snowdrop centrist; both are partially accurate descriptions. However, even these two do not fit comfortably on a scale of left to right. In Snowdrop, many would hardly have thought of themselves as left, centre or right. Rather, they were engaged in a politics with little reference to such divisions and drew support from across the political spectrum. The Patriot movement, especially in its racist, anti-semitic, homophobic, gun-totin' moments, seems classically neo-fascist. Yet at times, it also draws on small-community, self-managing principles that might have come from communitarian left groups. For example, an opposition to globalizing forces has been a bridge between what are often assumed to be left-wing anti-globalization activists and the far-right Patriot movement. There seems little doubt that during the anti-World Trade Organization protests in Seattle in 1999, neo-fascists opposed to the New World Order were a minority presence among anti-fascist, anti-globalization protesters. The contradictions here can be indicated by reports that anti-globalization neo-fascists attacked Black anti-globalization protesters. Noting such connections and contemplating their possibility is not a matter of smearing anti-globalization protesters as naïve or potential fascists, neither of which is the case. Instead, it is worth noting only as one indication among many that the political axis of left to right does not always help in understanding activism!.

This chapter has defined two questions that divide popular political activism in the 21st century into three broad groups. First, is a movement transgressive? Second, what relationship does a transgressive movement's core beliefs and ethics have to time? We are now in a position to jump into activism! and follow its politics. This can best be done not by exploring a list of campaigns or groups, but through four different themes: direct action and dis/organization, pleasure, culture jamming and hacktivism.

CHAPTER THREE

Action and Dis/Organization

Non-violent Direct Action and Dis/Organization

What actions do transgressive movements take? What demonstrations, blocked roads and unfurled banners do they create? What ethical visions can be found within the political actions of activism!? And, as each action is created, what roads must blocked, what dates set, what activists notified and mobilized and what banners furled before their day in the sun? What typical forms of co-ordination do activist!s develop?

Activism! is least visible when actions are being prepared and most visible when action is taken. It is always this combination of the hidden and the seen, of that which is hard to find and that which cannot be avoided. Mass protests, riots, civil disobedience, tunnels and tree-houses are the public face of activism!, the moments when activists try to make themselves and their ethics unavoidable. They may try to make themselves unavoidable in one event – for example, by infiltrating a shareholders' meeting – and may, at the same time, try to make themselves unavoidable to the whole of society – by creating an event that the media will broadcast. Activist!s alert us to genetically modified food, make us feel responsible for animal welfare and ensure that we know how little the workers who make our trainers are paid; and they make us aware that all of these things make some people very angry indeed. Such visibility depends on the less visible work of dis/organization, which involves networks of affection and commitment. While we will inevitably focus on the cutting edge of activism!, its most visible forms of action, we will also explore how movements co-ordinate and sustain themselves. The visible and the invisible depend on each other, even if the visible is what draws our eye.

To explore the multiplicity of actions taken by transgressive movements, I will take up two intersecting core principles: non-violence and direct action, or non-violent direct action (NVDA). It is not that all activist actions embody NVDA, or even that one definition of NVDA holds across activism!; rather, it is that non-violence and direct action are two sets of ideas through which activists constantly discuss and recreate action. This is both in the sense of defining what they mean by non-violence and direct action and defining themselves as for or against either non-violence or direct action. Neither are non-violence or direct action independent axes; they cannot easily be separated and have a tendency to blend into each other. However, it is possible to separate them analytically and even to imagine ideal actions that might embody one axis while radically minimizing the other. We will also see from analysis of these axes how activism! has continually solicited and refused violence. We will be able to understand how naked, physical aggression against both property and people may become less a matter of principle and more a matter of tactics. Activism! will show its ugly side as well. Following this we will turn to the invisible work of dis/organization.

NVDA: Non-violence

Though many activists now feel that sometimes interminable debates about violence or non-violence should be put in the past, it is important to explore them to grasp not just the most recent forms of activism! but its broad ethical basis. Non-violent protest has a number of traditions and a long history. In such actions as boycotts and strikes, we can find non-violent protests far back in history. It is not hard to understand this long lineage. Non-violent protests based on withdrawing co-operation both strike at the heart of society and sidestep any superior force the target might have. Workers' strikes operate with such principles. Simply refusing to work both hurts the employer and sidesteps much of the employer's usually greater legal and physical force. For the employer to recover, they have to reveal the threat they control and become violent themselves. For example, when some Polish shipyard workers went on strike and occupied their yards in 1970–71, the authorities met marches with bullets and, on a number of occasions, killed workers. The Soviet Union ordered no further firing into crowds of workers due to the political difficulties it caused; this led to both a change in leadership in the Polish state and negotiations with workers. Though these negotiations did not lead to the workers' main demands being met, they did lay some of the groundwork necessary to Solidarity's success in the 1980s. Non-violence is both an obvious and a necessary tactic of protest for those who are subject to greater physical force.

We also need to understand how non-violent protests are conceived in particular times and spaces. Simply to point to a long history and the obvious practical uses of non-violence hardly begins to explore its particular definitions. Is it non-violence against property? Or non-violence against people? While we should never lose sight of the practical nature of such protest, and it will be easy to be drawn into some of the more metaphysical conceptions of violence, we also need to explore how non-violence is both conceptualized and enacted. Otherwise, we cannot see the particular types of non-violent tactics that have entered activism!.

We can draw out most of the relevant key arguments by taking up one key source in Gandhi's ideas and their use in struggles against colonialism in India. Gandhi himself drew on prior examples and ideas, of course. For example, the particular attention he paid in his work to strikes associated with the 1905 uprisings in Russia proved a powerful resource for struggles that followed.[1] (The American civil-rights movement comes to mind here.) Taking up Gandhi's vision of non-violence allows us to cut to the heart of the question 'What does non-violence mean in activism!?'

It is the conception of *satyagraha* that allows us to move directly to ideas about non-violence. Variously translated as 'soul-force' or 'love-force', the notion of *satyagraha* was developed by Gandhi in campaigns first in South Africa and then in India. His idea was that non-violent and non-retaliatory resistance to oppression asserts a moral superiority over the oppressor. Those who practice *satyagraha* do two things. First, they demonstrate their moral superiority over their oppressors. This leads, Gandhi believed, to the oppressor realizing their own moral and spiritual failures and then giving way. Second, practitioners build their own spiritual position, because non-violence leads to truth. The goodness and morality of followers of *satyagraha* is constantly developed and demonstrated by practising *satyagraha*. Simultaneous with such metaphysical concerns is the act of non-violence – boycott, refusal to co-operate and so on – that provides practical teeth for *satyagraha*'s high ideals. In articulating non-violence in these ways, Gandhi codified non-violence and located its power.

Examples of these beliefs and tactics can be taken from the struggle to free India from colonial domination. In 1916, Gandhi and his colleagues began a major campaign by building on a traditional Indian form of protest, the *hartal*. This was a boycott in which all shops and workplaces closed, and people created public demonstrations of mourning to show disapproval. In this particular instance, Gandhi sought to harness a *hartal* to a campaign against laws that cracked down on protests against colonial domination (the Rowlett Acts). These particular protests ran out of what he saw as control, leading to violent riots and clashes with armed police.

A second campaign in the early 1920s saw Gandhi and the Congress Party calling on people to hand back titles and decorations given by the British, to withhold taxes, to remove children from government schools, to boycott elections, to ignore courts and more, all in an attempt to undo the colonial government. These non-violent protests were taken up in many parts of India. Rent was not paid, courts were ignored, government officials quit their jobs, and those who enforced government rule, such as the police, were ostracized. Of key importance was the salt-tax boycott. The taxing by the colonial government of this essential requirement of life was felt as an injustice by nearly all sectors of society. Protest was developed that both resisted paying the tax and encouraged people to make their own salt. For those with access to saltwater, an important way to resist was to boil the water away and collect the salt residue. This could then be sold, without tax being paid, used or simply passed around. Here, we see the practical side of non-violence, the provision of actions that anyone can take, actions that clearly address a widely perceived injustice and involve no physical violence. These actions also materially affected the oppressor, aiming to make India ungovernable. More generally, the suffering people brought on themselves by their non-violent resistance was meant to be the proof of their moral superiority through which the invaders would finally be vanquished.

There has been much criticism of *satyagraha*, especially of the purist forms in which Gandhi tended to propound it. For example, the gulf between his conception and the sometimes violent behaviour of fellow-demonstrators in his campaigns is often commented on. Yet for modern-day activist!s, two key principles flow from *satyagraha*. First, there is the interpretation of non-violence to include non-retaliation. In non-violent actions, protesters do not respond to whatever aggression is inflicted on them. In sit-ins, where people simply sit down in a place that blocks the workings of an opposition, it is common advice not to resist when police come to remove you, but simply to go as limp as you possibly can, making yourself as heavy a dead-weight as possible. Second, and perhaps more fundamentally, powerful consequences have resulted from the belief that non-violent protests demonstrating moral superiority can lead to social change. This may seem hopelessly idealistic, but it is the precursor of media strategies in which demonstrating moral superiority and having it broadcast to many people may change society. Making injustice and oppression public and unavoidable is one way of understanding *satyagraha*'s injunction to demonstrate moral superiority. Such demonstrations force others to decide if they can live with the moral deficit produced in themselves in the face of an unavoidable demonstration of what is better. Questioning the morality of a social practice in a way that reaches broadly through society in the hope of changing that social practice is closer to the seemingly idealist strategies of *satyagraha* than we may think. Gandhi was also operating, in some ways, with such a model, as he saw his demonstrations of the moral impossibility of colonialism in India as being partly aimed at British public opinion. This is a key point articulated by *satyagraha*. Non-violent actions need to connect to wider social forces to create the large-scale social change that is envisaged. All those who participated in the anti-salt-tax actions in India were aiming not just at the salt tax but at colonialism as well.

It is often asserted that such non-violent principles are naïve in comparison to the power of the state. However, we should remember that Gandhi also operated in an environment where death was present, not just the historical stench of colonialism's appetite for human destruction, but the death dealt out to protesters. For example, early in the development of widespread non-violent actions, 379 demonstrators were killed and fifteen hundred wounded when British troops opened fire on a peaceful meeting in Amritsar. For some, moments like these mark the end of non-violent action, but for others they signal a renewed commitment. Even extreme situations, Gandhi might have argued, reinforce *satyagraha*, because they demonstrate the moral superiority of the dead protester over the living oppressor in an extreme way. The news that the officer who ordered the

Amritsar massacre was treated as a hero in parts of Britain helped to convince many that colonialism had to end.

Demonstrating clearly and openly the moral superiority of one side of an argument is one way in which non-violence is used as a campaign tactic to this day. It is the connection between the violence of oppressors and the non-violence of protesters that establishes this moral position, though this is also a connection that has come under strain. Before touching on that strain, it will be useful to draw in a second source for non-violence in activism!: the Quaker notion of bearing witness.

While Gandhi's conception of non-violence, non-co-operation and non-retaliation has formed a key source for conceptions of non-violence in activism!, his is certainly not the only or the oldest conception of non-violence as a political and spiritual tactic. The Quakers developed similar notions in their belief in the need to 'speak truth to power' and to 'bear witness'. For them, the wrongs of the world need to be seen, to be brought into the light, both to accuse perpetrators and to ensure their visibility. 'Bearing witness' comes close to *satyaghara* in the connection drawn between non-violence and moral superiority. These concepts were taken up and articulated in political action, particularly in the Suffragette movement. Here, the injustice of repressing women, of keeping them secondary legally, morally, politically and economically, was confronted through numerous tactics. A key strand, especially in early struggles, was non-violence conceived within Quaker traditions. While non-violence was not the only tactic employed within the various organizations and events that made up the Suffragette movement, it was articulated in ways that were to connect, particularly, to early 1960s peace campaigns and into current activism!.

Introducing the Suffragettes opens out the influences of non-violence from *satyaghara* alone. Ideas have filtered through a number of movements, just as the Quaker tradition was taken up by both nineteenth-century feminism and twentieth-century peace activism. The American civil-rights movement, the peace and anti-nuclear movements and the post-1960s movements of feminism, gay and lesbian rights, Black power and green politics all continued to interrogate and develop non-violence. By the early 21st century, non-violence had developed into a complex political tactic, whose fundamental attraction continues to be the belief that it allows power to be unveiled, hopefully drawing in all who see the naked face of repression to oppose it. In societies saturated by media coverage and in which the possibilities for media production by grass-roots organizations have increased, the ability of non-violent protest to unveil the face of power has increased correspondingly. However utopian notions of bearing witness or *satyaghara* may appear, their strategy of creating social change through publicity begins to make more sense than ever before in the context of globalized, instantaneous communication. These ideas have also been developed in the context of modern activism! in a way that unpicks the previous equation of moral superiority with non-violence, opening the path to morally superior violence. To see this gradual separation of key terms of non-violent protest, we need to examine direct action.

NVDA: Direct Action

Non-violence only makes an impact when it is allied to public action. Non-violence's potential is only realized when there is action in which violence is a possible outcome. If there could never be violence, the choice to be non-violent would have no moral basis – that is, being non-violent would not prove the superiority of one social vision over another.

Like non-violence, direct action should not be thought of as a single tactic, but as a collection of ideas and actions which stretches from passive notions of civil disobedience to active, often aggressive, interventions. Some of the roots of direct action lie in civil disobedience, another form of action that has fed into non-violence and has powerfully articulated direct action itself. For example, Henry David Thoreau's classic essay 'Civil Disobedience' argues that a tactic like refusing to pay taxes is one way of asserting that it is morally necessary to disobey the laws of a corrupt or illegitimate government. Rather than asserting the moral superiority of the person performing a non-violent act, as Gandhi did, Thoreau focused on the moral superiority of the act – not what the individual *is*, but how they *do something*. There is a subtle difference between social change resulting from making your opponent face your moral superiority through non-violent acts and trying to bring down your opponent by acting against his/her immoral demands. It is a shift from the person and morality to the opponent and action. This distinction widens when we realize that civil disobedience, from its beginnings, did not develop any inherent attachment to non-violent over violent actions. Direct action means a shift to actions that stop what is wrong, rather than simply having faith that moral superiority will lead, somehow, to change. We can explore what this shift means by looking at the place of civil disobedience and direct action in societies that allow such protests.

In liberal democratic societies, in which demonstrations and civil disobedience are, within carefully policed limits, accepted, the ability to create moments in which power reveals itself becomes difficult. For reforming movements such as Snowdrop, this is not a problem. If anything, for reforming movements, being able to plan demonstrations in conjunction with state authorities is reassuring and adds to their sense of building within existing social institutions. But for movements seeking transgression, being restrained within approved avenues can be unacceptable.

The acceptance of protest by the state incorporates protest into the state; it presses the claims of the present against those of the future. One answer to this came from environmental protesters in the 1990s who developed what Brian Doherty has called 'manufactured vulnerability',[2] thus ensuring that transgression is possible within liberal democratic societies. Protesters attempt directly to affect a development by placing themselves into physically vulnerable situations. A protester attempting to prevent destruction of some woodland might dig a tunnel, deliberately not completely strengthening parts, and then lock themselves onto a concrete-filled drum sunk to the tunnel's bottom. This means that those contracted to build a road, airport or shopping mall over the woodland would have to be extremely careful in finding and removing the protester. Alternatively, a protester might build tree-houses and walkways in the sky. Living in a tree-house ensures that the activist cannot be surprised by the sudden destruction of the woodland, and tree-houses and walkways are difficult and dangerous to remove when protesters are in them and moving around. With these transgressions, we might feel that we are back to *satyaghara*, with demonstrators revealing their moral superiority through non-violent resistance. However, activists in these situations reject such an interpretation; they are not seeking coverage to call indirectly for change, but are doing what they can to prevent the natural environment being destroyed. They are taking direct action:

> London RTS [Reclaim the Streets] uses direct action. This is not, as many commentators would suggest, a clever technique to gain media exposure at a time when competition for space is intense. Direct action is about perceiving reality, and taking concrete action to change it yourself. It is about working collectively to sort out our own problems, doing what we thoughtfully think is the right course of action, regardless of what various 'authorities' deem acceptable. It is about pushing back the boundaries of possibility, about inspiration, empowerment. It is about thinking and taking, not asking and begging.[3]

Direct action seems as simple as its name. Activists take something that is happening in society that they object to and then try to prevent it. For example, in the UK in the 1990s, environmental activists drew on previous traditions of peace camps, particularly the women's camp at Greenham Common, which protested against the upgrading of nuclear missiles, and developed a number of camps that lay in the path of road developments. These included squatting houses in East London to prevent the development of a new motorway. This latter campaign included both ongoing invasions of road-construction sites, to delay work, and the building of obstacles to make it extremely difficult for evictions to occur. From a huge net strung high in the air to a barricaded basement, there were attempts to ensure that the motorway would be prevented. There were several similar camps in rural areas, such as those at Twyford Down or Newbury, both before and after the East London protest. In these camps, people took to living in tents and benders/teepees in the path of a planned road, ensuring both a constant opposition presence, often realized in invasions of construction sites and destruction of road equipment, and an obstacle that had to be removed before the road could continue. Police, security guards and construction workers had to confront ongoing protests. For example, within an invasion of a construction site, a demonstrator might climb to the top of a crane, thus preventing its use until the demonstrator was removed. In addition, set-piece battles had to occur to evict camps. It is true that direct actions utilizing manufactured vulnerability often produce symbolic moments that are highly attractive to mainstream media, whether through the spectacular nature of constructions or the drama of confrontation, but this is not necessarily their aim. Direct action does, however, accumulate the symbolic aspects of non-violence in this way while driving them further by adding the simple aim of making the world as the activists believe it should be.

Manufactured vulnerability forms a bridge between non-violence and direct action. We can see how such actions both create media spectacles in which activists uncover the morality of modern life and also attempt to alter that life directly. A complication of this fusion of non-violence and direct action is that it is sometimes difficult to see whether a direct action achieves its end. For example, in each of the road protests just mentioned, the road being opposed was, in fact, built. In each case, no matter how ingenious or committed activists were, they were beaten down through a combination of police and private-security muscle and the law. This does not mean that the activists were wasting their time or failed entirely. They came to realize that each direct action was raising the cost of subsequent construction and that, in the end, though they might not save one particular woodland, the struggle might save a woodland in the future. And the UK's road-building programme was curtailed by the late 1990s, though whether this was solely attributable to demonstrators is questionable.

Techniques with a similar spirit have developed among other activists. For example, some eco-activists in North America pioneered 'spiking', which involves driving spikes into trees so that any chainsaw used to try and cut a tree will hit metal and break. When portable metal-detecting or x-ray equipment was used by loggers to detect spikes, activists responded with x-ray-invisible ceramic spikes. This, in turn, prompted a debate, because ceramic spikes tended to splinter, damaging chain-saws but also endangering the workers using them. For some, such a direct action was justified in the defence of certain forests, while for others, the logger working in harsh conditions for a day's pay was clearly not the target and should not be put at risk. In a different register, the series of anti-globalization protests of the late twentieth and early 21st centuries were also based on direct-action principles. In Seattle, Prague, Quebec, Melbourne and Genoa, a meeting of a key 'neo-liberal globalization organization', such as the World Trade Organization or the World Bank, was targeted to be halted. Here, the direct actions sought to prevent various organizations from deepening the process of free-market globalization. Another example is that in a protest in the now-famous Chiapas Mountains of Mexico, indigenous women, bare-footed and with sticks, beat back invading Mexican army units. Such actions have had resonance for other indigenous peoples attempting to take control of land, prevent development or otherwise control their world, often in direct actions such as land seizures, communal defence of lands and destructive invasions of developments. Of course, the 1967 attempt to levitate the Pentagon failed, though it is perhaps a different class of direct action: the MDA, or mystical direct action.

In these examples, the focus of direct action shifted from demonstrating a morally superior position to taking action with others to create a better world. Despite many similarities between activist!s focused on non-violence or on direct action, there is a difference between actors and actions. And the focus on actions that re-make the world, as opposed to personal responsibilities that demonstrate how the world should be, unpicks commitments to non-violence and subjects violence to a re-categorization. The small difference I have noted widens so that violent direct action operates at the limit of activism!.

NVDA: Violence

Direct action's attempts to grab the world and shake it are informed by broad moral principles, but the nature of these actions does not itself constitute that morality. This means that in direct action, the means and the ends are not necessarily identified with each other. As direct action does not, in principle, endorse non-violence, we can see a way opening up to activist! violence. We can see how, despite a lineage of non-violent protests, modern activism! has been able to learn from this tradition while also separating non-violence from being an end in itself. Instead of non-violence being something necessary, it can become something tactical, and that means that violence is a possibility from within activism! – not a reaction to state violence, which is ever-present, but the adoption of violence by activist!s.

We can see this by exploring the protest in Prague in 2000, when thousands of activists gathered to oppose a meeting of the World Bank and International Monetary Fund. They pursued a strategy of trying to keep delegates trapped within the conference centre where the meeting was taking place, in contrast to Seattle in 1999, when activists had tried to prevent delegates reaching a meeting of the World Trade Organization. Activists achieved the Prague blockade by jamming entrances and forcing thousands of police to ring the building to prevent them from entering the conference centre. In effect, activists created a double ring around the centre: the inner ring made up of police, tanks and water-cannon, and the outer ring of activists. This led to delegates being trapped in the conference centre till late at night, meaning that their evening at the opera had to be cancelled. It also led to the conference being closed down early, after its second day. As one activist reporting on the events suggested:

> Despite the low turnout, the demonstrations and actions in Prague seem to have been almost as successful as Seattle in terms of shutting down the conference. There weren't actually enough people to blockade the entrances to the Conference Centre but what we lacked in numbers we made up for in violence.[4]

In this direct action, the broader morality – anti-neo-liberal globalization – fuelled a series of actions whose aim (or end) was to shut down a meeting for the proponents of the particular economic programme. Within these actions, the means were subordinate to the end. Here, the debate between violent and non-violent actions, often called spiky and fluffy respectively, lost its overriding moral imperative and came down to whether violence or non-violence was effective or not. Such debates begin to take on a functional air instead of the theological importance that discussions of *satyaghara* often have. Here are some further reflections on Prague from a different activist:

We never collectively discussed or thought about exactly what we were trying to do on S26 in Prague . . . Basically, if we as a group were going to do anything more than sit in the road as a blockade, and actually try and get in the Conference Centre for example, then (short of some fantastically clever plan that nobody had) we were going to need to use some sort of violence to do it. And for this to be as effective as possible, and for us to avoid as much risk to ourselves as possible, it needed to some extent to be pre-planned and co-ordinated . . . However, to attempt to raise this before the 26th in the planning of the action would have been incredibly divisive, as large numbers . . . would have strongly disagreed . . . It's one thing to defend, or at least not condemn, spontaneous violence in self-defence, or to get everyone to agree that property damage is okay, but quite another to sit down and pre-plan a violent attack on the police.[5]

We can see within these reflections on Prague how non-violence becomes a technical issue related to the success or failure of the action and does not function as a principle in its own right. This is one example of the way in which the development of direct action during the 1980s and '90s in some movements gradually minimized debates around the morality of non-violence in favour of its efficacy. In particular, violence against property has become accepted as a component of direct actions, whether it is raiding a construction office and destroying its computers or, as happened in 2001, torching the four-wheel-drives in an American 'sport utility vehicle' dealership because such vehicles are environmentally destructive. Violence against people has remained more controversial, in both the senses of reacting to aggression and of deliberately planning to attack people. At this point, activism! opens a door not just to all kinds of violence but to terrorism. The emblematic activist organization here might be the Animal Liberation Front (ALF), which has been held responsible for some 'terrorist' actions, as well as being a component of the far wider pool of activists, actions and organizations that make up animal-liberation struggles and that, in the main, utilize NVDA.

Two offshoots of the ALF, The Justice Department and the Animal Rights Militia, have taken stances extending violence to property and people. In one instance in 1994, six letter-bombs were sent to companies involved in exporting live animals in Europe, placing both property and human life in danger. Gurj Aujla, who pleaded guilty to sending the bombs, argued:

> This wasn't token protest, or mindless retribution, or even economic sabotage . . . it was strategic action. I researched that the meat trade is massive and can't be easily beaten, but live export is one vulnerable aspect of that trade that could be defeated. Furthermore, the ferry companies are not primary animal abusers, they could exist perfectly well without live exports, so hit them and they will withdraw – and they did.[6]

Again, we can see how violence can become a technical element in a direct action, even including violence against people. We have reached a point as far from the principles of non-violence as we can possibly be, in which activists view violence against property or people as a viable tactic depending on its efficacy. This does not mean that elements of non-violent beliefs, like *satyaghara,* are no longer present; for example, the strategy of creating wide appeal through spectacular actions that attract media attention may remain.

We have seen how violence is part of a debate within activism!, which, even if it does not lose its commitment to non-violent principles, is also subject to pressures towards violence. Even with this critical point in mind, it is also clear that NVDA offers not so much a recipe for taking action as a *smörgåsbord* from which activist!s can develop actions. With these thoughts in mind it is now time to move on because, as already stated, action cannot exist without preparation and co-ordination. Some people have to choose the target, think of why they are targeting, choose the means of action, choose the date and so on. These are all part of the far less visible times in which co-ordination happens. Though it is in action that political effects are created, it is preparation that allows action to occur.

Dis/Organization: Anti-hierarchies and Hidden Hierarchies

In relation to past and expected future press reports concerning trials of RTS 'leaders', Reclaim the Streets London would like to emphasise that it is a non-hierarchical, leaderless, openly organised, public group. No individual 'plans' or 'masterminds' its actions and events. RTS activities are the result of voluntary, unpaid, co-operative efforts from numerous self-directed people attempting to work equally together.[7]

Activism! employs certain forms of co-ordination that are often called dis/organization. These forms, as indicated by RTS's statement, oppose the kind of hierarchical and bureaucratic codes of organization that are most often met in society. It is against these codes or norms that activism! has developed dis/organization.

The core component of dis/organization is a commitment to open organizing using flat hierarchies. Flat networks for co-ordination mean allowing all who want to participate to do so. Flat hierarchies are an ethical statement. They are a belief that all who participate in a dis/organization have something (not necessarily the same thing) to contribute and that forms of co-ordination must strive to draw all the worth they can from everyone's contribution. In practice, this means ensuring open access to all co-ordinating meetings, as well as leaving space for spontaneous reinterpretation of actions. If a co-ordination network is truly flat, there is no privileged decision-making point; instead, at any moment, a decision can be revisited by those involved. While this seems on the face of it to remove all notion of co-ordination from dis/organization, it ensures that the decisions taken do not strangle improvisation. Flat hierarchies are, ideally, based on direct communication between all participants and are facilitated through open meetings that all interested parties can attend. Different articulations of dis/organization develop using different interpretations and implementations of these elements. Within dis/organization, a powerful commitment to certain forms of co-ordination and an alternative form of social organization is articulated.

These are some of the ideals, the principles, that dis/organizations seeks to put into practice. As has been known for some years among activists, these principles are less than perfectly realized, and flat hierarchies tend to hide bumps. Within feminism, this was discussed as the 'tyranny of structurelessness'. Tyrannies may result from different arenas privileging different skills. For example, open meetings require the confidence to speak in public, as well as rewarding articulate speakers. Informal networking in cafés and bars, or after meetings, requires both charm and the ability to be present; going out after a meeting for a drink is not an option for all, particularly those with family responsibilities. The different skills needed for these different moments of co-ordination can underpin the emergence of implicit hierarchies, as can other intangible factors such as history within a group, charisma or the sheer amount of time someone may devote to a group. These can produce hills in what should be flat plains. Another way of seeing difficulties is to note that the flip-side to the strengths some have are the weaknesses others have, either in the particular skills needed for meetings of different sorts or in less formal networking. Just as strengths create hills in flat hierarchies, so weaknesses may produce troughs.

For example, Reclaim the Streets has, at times, enforced media silence on some members that the group felt were speaking too often in public and so gaining too high a profile. It was believed that such members, not necessarily through their own desire for power, were becoming recognized as leaders. On the one hand, such a move could be seen as highly principled, removing experienced volunteers in order to maintain a principled equality. On the other hand, it could be seen as perversely self-damaging, both insulting highly committed figures who are treated as power-mongers and removing those who had proved themselves best able to handle such tasks. The reality of dis/organization can be seen in such confused, principled and damaging moments.

A further common example of co-ordination within dis/organizational principles is affinity groups. These draw on the history of anarchist organization and more recent use in protests such as those against dams in Australia in the 1980s. The New York branch of the radical direct-action Aids organization ActUp! has noted:

Affinity groups are self-sufficient support systems of about 5 to 15 people. A number of affinity groups may work together toward a common goal in a large action, or one affinity group might conceive of and carry out an action on its own. Sometimes, affinity groups remain together over a long period of time, existing as political support and/or study groups, and only occasionally participating in actions.[8]

Affinity groups may be the building blocks of large dis/organizations or may operate on their own. They may be focused on protest, education or support. Their essence lies in the personal care a small group of people who know each other and meet regularly can offer one another. This is particularly useful when planning direct action that involves confrontation. Affinity-group members support each other during an action and perform the vital role of checking where everyone is at the end it, something that can often lead to checking police stations or, in worst cases, hospitals. The confidence given by knowing that someone is going to do such things can make many people more committed in direct actions. But, as ActUp note, affinity groups may function outside confrontational direct actions. They may feed into larger dis/organizations with each affinity group putting their positions forward. They may also simply function as collective education projects, for example as reading groups.

This all sounds neatly egalitarian and like a way of managing both large and small co-ordinations along dis/organizational principles. Yet again, the principles reveal themselves to be two-sided. What mechanisms are there for small groups to feed into larger groups? If there are demonstrations of tens of thousands of people, there may be thousands of affinity groups. While each group may function well internally, it is often the case that overall decisions disappear either into an endless discussion, in which reporting back to affinity groups must go on continually, or into a failure to even make decisions, leaving action up to the whim of particular moments. While the commitment to dis/organization can be admired, it can also be less than efficient.

Affinity groups offer a concrete example of dis/organized co-ordination. Dis/organization has costs alongside the benefits we have been looking at. In particular, they must be constantly open not only to lengthy inclusive discussions, but also to reopening them. The sheer time and effort required by dis/organization, especially if one becomes quite large, can make it unwieldy. Meeting burn-out is not uncommon among activists, and dis/organization activists may be more prone to it than others. The uncertainty of decision-making and the length of time needed to reach consensus are clear potential drawbacks. The final problem has already been touched on in the emergence of invisible or hidden organization within dis/organization.

Dis/Organization: The Future and Utopia

In the face of such difficulty of co-ordination, we might well wonder whether some more formal, even organizational, means might not be appropriate. In particular actions, this may well be true. But there is a general point about dis/organization that perhaps makes clear why it is of value to activism! despite its failings. What is key about dis/organization is not just the way it puts principles of equality and justice into action, but that in doing so it brings a little of the future into the present. Dis/organization is a prefigurative politics, because it attempts to preview what social change may bring. In being dis/organized, activists begin to act as if the world they want to live in has come into existence. Prefigurative politics means acting now as you want to act in the future.

Here is one example of affinity groups and prefigurative politics coming together in the middle of a demonstration. At the demonstrations in Prague against the IMF and the World Bank, there were three separate marches. One was called the pink and silver, as those colours – along with black – predominated in the crowd. A decision-making procedure was developed to allow a dis/organized two-thousand-person march. At the centre of the march were a number of people with walkie-talkies and mobile phones. These were in communication with a mobile and a static command centre, who were, in turn, in communication with a number of outriders on bikes who were scouting out possible directions. There was a big pole at the head of the march, and flags run up it indicated the direction. This permitted co-ordination, but decisions still had to be taken. The march was organized into affinity groups, and each group had a delegate. When a decision was needed, the delegates had to meet, go back to their affinity group and then return to make the decision. As one participant said,

> Using this unwieldy process we just about managed to walk down the road in the same direction together (although sometimes it

was touch and go when we hit a corner) and to be subject to this command structure on the day was one of the most disempowering and frustrating experiences of my political life.[9]

And, not surprisingly, this cumbersome procedure barely lasted past the first confrontations with the police. Here, a strong commitment to principles of dis/organization led not to the inclusion and empowerment such prefigurative politics aim at, but, at least for this participant, to the opposite. Even given these failures, this example allowed the development of some dis/organization. It allowed the future to be tested and found wanting and alternatives to emerge.

Dis/organization should not be thought of simply as an inclusive, democratic, slow and fragile means of co-ordinating political actions and education but also as an ethical time machine. It might even be that dis/organization, for all of its often unwieldy forms of co-operation and hidden failures, is important because it makes the future begin. In so many ways, activists may become obsessed with their present – the next demonstration, the next meeting, the next email, the next book. By embedding an ethics of the future – ideally democratic, grass-roots, open and equal – within the means by which actions are conducted, activism! ensures that its focus on the future is not lost even amid timescales as short as the next hour and day. Dis/organization is a hidden future inside the present.

Activism!: Tute Bianche

To conclude discussions of non-violent direction action and dis/organization, we can take up a particular example and see in it both innovative re-articulations of NVDA and inter-relations between action and dis/organization. Looking at another march from the Prague demonstration, we can see the tactics employed as a novel, though again flawed, attempt to rework NVDA.

To begin, we need to circle back and reassert non-violence and its importance. The vast majority of activism! employs non-violent direct actions, utilizing all of the principles that have been discussed above. Activists open up alternative views within these debates, drawing participants in different directions: towards media events demonstrating moralities; towards directly changing some part of the world; towards violence or non-violence. NVDA is a series of lines of argument that swing constantly around two axes. One axis runs from non-violence as a moral principle, as the means and end of actions, to violence as a tactic, as a means to an end. The other axis runs from indirectly changing the world through spectacular events that demonstrate the necessity of change to directly changing one component of the world to effect social change, there and then. These are abstract positions; in the reality of activism! they merge and blend. We can see such blending in the emergence of a tactic developed by related Italian groups Tute Bianche (white overalls) and Ya Basta! and imitated by the English group, the Wombles, and the Australian group the Wombats.

This tactic is relevant to mass demonstrations and involves attaching all manner of protection to an activist's body: foam rubber, inner tubes, helmets, padded gloves. Over all of this padding, activists wear white overalls to symbolize the invisibility of marginalized peoples. Once a group are 'padded up', they work in a demonstration acting as a buffer between police and protesters, or by linking arms and pressing against police lines. Activists are largely protected by their padding from blows by the police, and with large numbers pushing, the aim may be to gradually burst open a police line or to protect demonstrators from police attacks. These tactics, generated by Tute Bianche and receiving world-wide publicity from their participation in the Prague demonstrations, were copied by others, for example in the May Day anti-capitalism protest in London. There, the Wombles (White Overalls Movement Building Libertarian Effective

Struggles) padded up and pushed through police lines. One activist offered this account:

> Our first confrontation was in Cavendish Sq . . . The police formed a line in riot gear. We were a little shaky, but basically walked up to them, arms linked behind the big blue tarp. They did their usual baton run, but with the protection we had on we could take it, and then pushed forwards and . . . blimey we were through the line! Wonderful feeling. After that whenever we came across more cops it was 'Wombles to the front.'. . . My glasses were knocked off, and I nearly got knocked down myself a few times so ended up very shaky, but kept up. I took some baton blows, but caught them all on my protected arm and was absolutely fine. Other Wombles took direct blows to their shins, arms and even heads and apart from some minor grazes we're all fine.[10]

The effect of padding up should not be overestimated. In Prague, Tute Bianche failed to breach police lines. In London, the Wombles breached a number of police lines, but thousands of demonstrators were still encircled and trapped by thousands of police for eight hours or more. In protests in Genoa in the summer of 2001 against the G8, the Tute Bianchi planned a major white-overalls intervention, including a large shield to be pushed at the head of the march. However, strong and early police attacks saw the tactic fail and widespread street fighting result. The justification for padding up is not just to facilitate direct action like closing the Prague conference but to remain close to non-violent principles of demonstrating who the oppressor is. A member of Tute Bianchi explains:

> For years our practice of self-defence has been instrumentalised by the media. Every time the police charged a legitimate and

peaceful march or demonstration, it was always [our] fault ... The papers would carry headlines like 'violence returns to the streets' ... We realized that the communication of events often modifies things more than the events themselves. We decided to send strong images and signals that left no doubts as to intentions. So we invented, rummaging through ancient history, systems of protective apparel, like plexiglass shields used tortoise-style, foam rubber 'armour', and inner-tube cordons to ward off police batons. All things that were visible and clearly for defensive purposes only. We wanted people to understand on which side lay reason, and who had started the violence. When we decide to disobey the rules imposed by the bosses of neo-liberalism, we do it by putting our bodies on the line, full stop. People can see images on the TV news that can't be manipulated: a mountain of bodies that advances, seeking the least harm possible to itself, against the violent defenders of an order that produces wars and misery. And the results are visible, people understand this, the journalists can't invent lies that contradict the images; last but not least, the batons bounce off the padding.[11]

Padding up is a way of ensuring that the police are blamed for violence and that demonstrators' discipline and non-violence are undeniable. Along the axes of direct to indirect action and violence to non-violence, Tute Bianche has created a tactic that simultaneously enacts all. The linked, padded activists march into violence. The police can be expected to try to hold their lines with all the force they can muster and will batter the padded Michelin-Man-like activists as much as they can. This tactic both ensures violence against people and is carried out non-violently. The violence inherent in the police and security forces is elicited and made visible. As seen at Prague, these tactics can serve to create spectacle and to directly affect the world.

We can now see dis/organization in the Tute Bianchi at Prague. So how did they get themselves and their padding there in the first place?

s26 in Prague was the first important occasion to send a signal in Europe of a real resistance to the plans of globalised capital. Ya Basta and Tute Bianche were involved from last summer in the meetings held in Prague to organize the demonstrations and direct actions (by the way, some of the Italians were rejected at the Czech border because they had taken part in these meetings) . . . We decided to reach Prague by train, given the large number of people involved. We had done this for earlier Euro-demonstrations in Amsterdam and Paris, 'squatting' a thousand seats in a train and affirming our right to freely demonstrate wherever in Europe. This time we didn't want to spend most of our energy in defending our right to leave, so we negotiated an agreement with the railways and we paid a nominal 'political price' to get a train for Prague.[12]

Here, we can see intermingled cultures of co-ordination and resistance. Taking the train with enough committed activists allows a different attitude to ticket prices than most of us are used to. Even with this brief example, we can see that – as we would expect – behind specific actions there are dis/organizational structures. Co-ordination in activism! involves opposition to what are perceived to be 'normal' means of organizing. Dis/organization is not only the means by which activism! lives in its hidden times; it is also how it transgresses widely accepted social codes of administration.

These actions and dis/organizations should also not be thought of as static. We have seen how the failure of some dis/organizational principles on the Pink and Silver march at Prague led to later reflections on just what appropriate forms of co-ordination should be on a confrontational march.

Similarly, as we have seen, Tute Bianchi planned a major march as part of the protests against the meeting of the G8 in Genoa in 2001. But their march met with immediate and violent clashes with the police, and extensive preparations by the city and state authorities led to the collapse of the Tute Bianchi's fine tactics. On the violent streets of Genoa, where one protester died, it was not possible to see Tute Bianchi as non-violent once their march had been disrupted and street fighting had become the response. The state, in effect, managed to prevent Tute Bianchi demonstrating according to their principles. This led to reflection and discussion, which led, in turn, to a recognition that 'padding up' may be a fine idea in principle but be unworkable in practice, possibly contributing to the running down of Ya Basta and the Tute Bianchi in Italy. Action and dis/organization are often contradictory and difficult, leading to unforeseen events and later reflection.

However, Tute Bianchi remains a powerful example, as in this one tactic all of the different elements of NVDA and dis/organization in activism! are at play, contradicting and complementing each other. More broadly, activism! tries to enact its futures through widely divergent tactics – spiking trees, torching cars, anti-hierarchies, sitting in, padding up, affinity groups – but all actions map onto the two axes of violence to non-violence and indirect to direct action, and all co-ordinations are run through the principles of dis/organization. *Satyaghara*, civil disobedience and all of the tactics of dis/organization and resistance that transgressive activists have employed are recreated within this nexus of possible actions. All of this history is swept up to be reinvented or enacted anew.

CHAPTER FOUR

Pleasure as a State Crime

We must make of joy once more a crime against the state.
Barney Hoskyns[1]

Pleasures, Moments, Politics

Moments of collective culture pass quickly. No sooner does a type of music enjoyed in a certain setting associated with particular clothes, drugs and attitudes become recognized as a collective endeavour than it changes. Even more ephemeral are the politics such pleasures of the moment generate. Whereas punk once seemed political, now it exists as a form of fashion. Sometimes, when such cultures are closely associated with an oppressed community and create representations for that community, as may be the case with rap and some African-American peoples, then the two – politics and pleasures – may be joined. Here, collective pleasures become political by being connected to a politics and not by being a politics in themselves. While rap is sometimes thought of as part of the struggle of African-Americans, and mods or rockers have been seen as manifestations of working-class youth, neither are, when considered politically, recognized as political in themselves. Pleasure as politics is most often understood in this way, as a contribution to movements that are defined by other criteria than that applied to sounds, dances and cultures. There are, of course, many moments of pleasure that it would be seem foolish to consider agents of social change; think of the New Romantics, of Marilyn Manson devotees, of Goths or of Spice power. Often, the pleasures of the body – aural, visual, sensual – that are vital components of such cultural moments are thought to have little political importance in their own terms and only register as moments of social change when they express a political wrong, such as poverty or repression, that is located elsewhere. Activism!, though, has overthrown this separation of politics and pleasure. The future has to feel good.

To begin to understand how pleasure has been integrated into activism! as a form of social change in itself, and why pleasure is an important element of these new ethics, we need to separate out two different understandings of pleasure and politics. First, there is the familiar notion of pleasure as a vehicle for politics. Here, we find music, dance, party and image all utilized to support activism. In some cases, the particular cultural form might seem integral to the politics, but in most it is coincidental. In either case, when looked at closely, the politics are pursued through the pleasure rather than being the pleasure itself. This can be seen most clearly in the benefit concert, when performers create pleasure in anticipation of the reward of donations to a political cause. In such cases, there is no necessary connection between politics and pleasure; there may even be a contradiction. For example, the Live Aid concerts were staged to generate money to feed starving people. The concerts consisted of performances by some of the most indulgent and excessive members of Western societies, rock and pop musicians. There is a deep contradiction between the excesses embodied in drummer Phil Collins, who played in Wembley Stadium and was then rushed via Concorde across the Atlantic to perform in the American Live Aid concert, and the desperate needs of starving peoples. Live Aid embodied the deep contradiction in many benefit concerts between the content of the pleasure and the meaning of the politics.

The second way pleasure has become integrated into activism! is pleasure as politics. This is often harder to understand, because it is all too easy to revert to separating pleasure from politics – that is, to finding an external 'cause' served by the pleasure. However, sets of relations have emerged between sound, lights, drugs, time, bodies and space that form a politics of its own. This second, sometimes fleeting and often hidden form is pleasure as politics or pleasure-politics. These two views – pleasure and politics versus pleasure-politics – must be explored in order to separate them. We can do this by briefly reliving two moments in the history of the worldwide youth and music movement usually called raving. These two moments introduce us to quite different sorts of politics that involve similar pleasures and in doing so help clarify how pleasure can be protest.

Rave On

The route to one rave in 1992 began with a phone number in *RaveScene* magazine, which led to an answering machine that advised tuning in to a pirate radio station at a certain time. At midnight, the radio station gave the meeting place as a railway station in the countryside. Once at the station, ravers were directed to wait until about twenty cars were ready, then a convoy was led off. An account of the night continues:

> After a while, we were driving through an industrial estate and out from the shadows appeared two crusties, directing us into a warehouse. It was very efficient, I mean in thirty seconds or less, the roller doors were up, the cars were in and the industrial estate was back to 1am silence.[2]

Once inside, the cars drove around for a while, trying to avoid the pillars holding up the roof, and parked. Several convoys arrived, taking different routes to try and ensure that the police were not alerted. Ten thousand watts of music power then ensued, the collective delirium of a rave in the empty offices, staircases and warehouse of a failed manufacturing industry.

In early 1995, there was an anti-roads demonstration in Camden, London. One element of the demonstration began the night before, at a rave organized by some of those working on the demonstration. The rave continued until dawn and then moved by public transport to Camden Town. Ravers did not know where they were going, but simply boarded the Underground and were told when to get off. Just outside the Underground station at Camden is an intersection of five roads near a shopping area and a well-known market. These shops attract a young audience and are invariably busy, so when the ravers appeared from the Underground dancing, whistling and banging drums, they were in a friendly place. Within a short space of time, several cars entered the intersection and were deliberately crashed by their demonstrator-drivers, paralyzing traffic in all five directions. Simultaneously, the road was invaded by the dancing crowd; jugglers, performers and food and drink tables all materialized on the street. Soon, a bicycle-powered generator arrived, music began and the rave restarted. Passers-by were invited to help demolish the crashed cars, and drivers stuck in the traffic jam were offered refreshments and leaflets. With numbers quickly swelling from the Sunday shoppers, this became a difficult demonstration to disperse, so the police took to redirecting traffic. In this precise, well-planned and successful demonstration, the pleasures of the rave served the politics, in preparing and conducting the demonstration.

Here, we see both pleasure-politics and pleasure and politics in action. In the warehouse, the pleasure of the rave is constructed in secret – pleasure for itself. In Camden, the pleasure of the rave helped to construct the demonstration – pleasure with politics. But what is the same and what is different here? Pleasure infuses both. Pleasure of drugs, of sweat, of psychedelic mind and hard-housed, pumping bodies, but what politics, what activism!, infuses them?

We can start an answer by asking 'What is rave?' In the mid–late 1980s, a number of trends in music, disco and party came together. These were, roughly, threefold. First, there was the development in the late 1970s and '80s within gay night life of a kind of ecstatic disco that combined lavish surroundings, high-energy music and certain drugs (with Ecstasy making an appearance) within environments that were both 'out' – that is, openly homosexual – and safe. Second, within African-American dance and night-life cultures, experiments with European 'techno' music and ways in which DJ's could build and control moods in discos were crossing over with different drugs, again including Ecstasy, and existing cultures of all-night parties. Finally, the former two trends crossed over and clashed with party cultures in the Balearic Islands, particularly Ibiza. Holidaying party-goers from Britain brought with them experiences with British-based, Jamaican-inspired sound systems and a do-it-yourself ethos derived from punk. The intermixing of these three themes, and myriad other smaller influences, resulted – in the UK and then world-wide – in a type of party/disco that depended on the construction of an ecstatic collective body.[3]

Raving became a constellation of music, drugs, youth, dancing, law evasion, fashion and money. At a rave event, people – sometimes tens of thousands, sometimes tens – dance all night, usually to some variant of 'techno' music, in a venue often fitted with a lightshow and with many people taking drugs, usually Ecstasy. The possible combinations of dance, lights, drugs, clothes, music and time create a collective delirium so that people literally 'rave'. What can be understood as the unifying or defining element of raving is this ongoing inducement into a desubjectified state of something like rapture. This desubjectification results in two key experiences, either feeling totally one with others in the dancing crowd or feeling totally alone dancing in a disconnected bubble. As Hillegonda Rietveld experienced it, 'Egos melt in the sweltering, frenzied heat of the mass of sweating bodies.'[4] Ravers may no longer notice the lights, the other ravers or the music as separate elements, but feel them as the one intense event.

However, raving is (was?) not simply these pleasures experienced in one event. It was also the sense of belonging many individuals felt across a series of different rave events and organizations. The collective pleasure was constructed and reconstructed at different, individual events, but such discrete moments were also recognized as part of some larger, encompassing movement. One raver claimed,

> On Friday night I went to a night club in London and the next day, Saturday, I went to a gig in Bristol but the amazing thing was that they were the *same place*: I recognised it not only as the same place but they were also the *same time* . . . In any conventional fashion, the two dance floors could not be in the same place at the same time but it was more that the place that the *trance* took me *was the same*. Both times I was transported through trance-dance.[5]

These events multiplied and proliferated across the world from the late 1980s. Sometimes, they were huge pay events, taking in thousands of people, sometimes they were small and free, and often they were somewhere in between the grandiose and the minor.

Let us return to the first of our two moments: the night-time run to a secret rave. This was part of what can be called the 'turn to secrecy'. Beginning in 1988, ravers in the UK had to confront a combination of tabloid outrage and police action that sought to directly repress a seemingly free-wheeling multiplication of rave events. Rather than engaging in direct confrontation, raves continued, but often became secret and were held in isolated places, directions to which could only be obtained through informal networks such as a friend or an anonymous telephone number.

A rave event might then occur completely hidden from public view. However, if the police found out and tried to prevent a secret event, a night of ravers trying to slip past police roadblocks would follow. Little 'normal' political action was taken to justify their pleasures. Ravers simply carried on trying to find more ingenious ways of fleeing the police and disappearing from public view. Hemment has noted the ongoing war to construct raving in Blackburn between 1989 and 1990, when raves attracted up to twelve thousand people, but were also secret:

> It was a continual struggle between party-goers and police, each side trying to outwit the other. A different location would be used each week. And new equipment would have to be constructed or acquired to replace that confiscated the week before . . . Like an Amazonian flower, Boomtown was only visible once a week, surviving the rest of the time as an underground network of roots that had no leader but constituted a flat meshwork . . . You can't arrest what you can't see.[6]

The decentralized networks that created and sustained this flight to secrecy were unified into a movement by the collectively recreated experience of delirium or ecstasy. This was a politics of the body and senses. At the centre of raving was a continually reconstructed collective body, the ecstatic flesh of ravers, around which revolved multiple organizations, ideas, events and individuals.

It was pleasures such as these that were also integrated into protest street parties, where the sudden sound of techno music booming across a public protest was often the easily understood signal for a party to begin amid the politics. In such cases, pleasure can be said to serve politics. For example, having a party the night before a demonstration is a way of ensuring that a good group of people, unified by their night-time experiences, will be present at the beginning of the demonstration.

There are two ways of understanding the place of pleasure in protest. First, there is pleasure itself, pleasure as transgression, pleasure as state crime. Second, there is the integration of pleasure into more obvious forms of protest to fuel and support them; while the pleasure and the protest might be linked, it remains clear that they are not the same thing. The latter is the most widely enacted connection between pleasure and politics (the benefit concert has been utilized by every conceivable politics from Live Aid to local anarchist groups). Pleasure and politics can easily be integrated into our previous discussions of action and dis/organization; pleasure becomes simply another element in these visible and invisible moments of activism!. Pleasure as politics, being more transgressive, remains harder to grasp as a political phenomenon.

The State Crime of Pleasure

Let us stay with rave as the core example and try to see how such pleasures of the dance floor may not only serve politics but be politics. Rave emerged into a political context dominated by the conservative politics variously known as Reaganism or Thatcherism. In its development of a hedonistic movement with a belief in the positive powers of those modern demons, drugs, raving can be seen as a radical cultural repudiation of modern conservatism. The right-wing governments of the 1980s and '90s took up not just legislative but also hegemonic political projects. They worked not only at widening the gap between rich and poor, poking larger and larger holes in the welfare state, but also at restructuring cultural values. Perhaps most potently, these governments often attempted to recreate senses of national identity, redefining what it meant to be British or American. One of the strands of this attempted reconstruction by conservatives was the identification of the 1960s as the time when 'things' went wrong, when far too liberal a regime achieved dominance. Within this context, raving can be understood as implicitly (sometimes explicitly) attacking the values of dominant political formations.

Raving transgressed hegemonic norms such as the rejection of drugs, addiction to hard work and preference for the individual over the communal. The politics we can draw from raving in and after 1988 can best be described as cultural, as a preference for transgression through symbols and pleasures rather than through protests and petitions. The naming by ravers of that year as the 'second summer of love' (after 1968) symbolizes raving's pleasure as a politics of cultural transgression. This is true even though rave's pay parties embraced entrepreneurial cultures created by conservatism. Those organizing huge events with the aim of profiting from them complained, when legislative and police crackdowns ensued, that they, the entrepreneurs of rave, were simply acting on the conservative call for innovation in profit making. These conservative economic attitudes within rave were ignored by conservatives themselves in an attempt to crush the cultures of pleasure.

Melucci has called this a process of challenging codes. As our societies are increasingly dominated by and created through information coming to us through proliferating means – more TV and radio channels, satellite, Internet, pagers, mobile phones, Internet-enabled mobile phones, Internet-enabled televisions – the information codes that create our world are playing increasingly important roles. Challenging such codes is exactly what pleasure achieved in rave, not in relation to information, but in relation to the creation of well-regulated selves. The conservative attempt to recreate what it meant to be British or American by imbuing this identity with traits of hard work, self-denial, certain legitimate racial characteristics and so on was attacked by the multiplicity, hedonism and hybridities achieved in rave and its events. What we can see is that it is pleasure itself, and, in particular, the twin pleasures of the body and of playing with symbols, that forms a politics of raving.

Of course, rave is not the first, nor will it be the last, such movement.

From at least the time of the hippies' adoption of drugs and sex as essential moments of rebellion (and almost certainly before that) through to the pleasures of the post-rave generations, activism!s have constantly been tied up with pleasure. Though it would be misleading to reduce gay and lesbian activisms to sexual pleasures, clearly an important component of their struggles is the desire to free desires from repression. A key element of second-wave feminism has been the reclamation, some would say reinvention, of female pleasure outside patriarchal oppressions. Some eco-activism has explored the pleasures of being in non-urban surroundings, both rural and wild environments, and of spiritual pleasures, particularly in pagan and neo-pagan beliefs. Thus pleasures of bodies and symbols abound within activism!.

Pleasure-politics

As with other aspects of activism!, it is not a matter of producing a single category or definition that pins down exactly what activist! pleasure is, like a butterfly collector pinning down a rare species. Rather, it is a matter of defining a number of axes whose intersections map out a field of pleasure-political action. There are three of these: pleasure as identity, the self-definition of pleasure, and articulation through repression. As with all such analytical divisions of activism!, the three axes should not be thought of as operating separately in a world where pleasure is lived; rather, they delineate activism!'s pleasures analytically. To see lived reality amid dead abstractions, I will continue mainly to use the pleasures of the dance floor as an example, for it is there that politics may seem most absent, yet activism! may be found.

In one sense, what we find in pleasure-politics is an inarticulate politics. It is a politics lived through touch, sound and sensation that is betrayed when it is articulated into speech or text. Images or sounds can sometimes convey the sensual appeals of pleasure-politics, but even so, the central affective connections will be missing. Of course, such affective elements are always present in social movements. They are usually bound up with a movement's collective identity; affection is part of the construction of the collectively lived political identity of activists. Melucci has put it this way:

> Passions and feelings, love and hate, faith and fear are all part of a body acting collectively, particularly in those areas of social life that are less institutionalised, such as social movements. To understand this part of collective action as 'irrational', as opposed to parts that are 'rational' (a euphemism for 'good'), is simply nonsensical. There is no cognition without feeling and no meaning without emotion.[7]

Melucci has pointed out how there is an emotional dimension in all social movements. His terminology allows us properly to articulate the unique collective identity in pleasure-politics, because in such politics meaning does not exist with emotion – *meaning is emotion*. In pleasure-politics, cognition does not include feeling, but *is* feeling. The essential component of a collective identity of a pleasure-politics is based not partially but totally on an all-consuming form of affectivity. For example, in the early 1990s, a rave scene developed in San Francisco, particularly around some full-moon parties held on beaches. A promoter, Jason Walker, remembered:

> The day of a full moon is a very heavy day for energy. Like Druid, pagan magic day, right? Celebrate the Mother. Lunar tides pulling and everything. I remember one Full Moon at Grey Whale Cove on Santa Cruz beach. As everyone started coming up on their Ecstasy, a huge ring formed around the DJ. Thousands of people

holding hands running circle, spinning. To me, it was like going back to witchcraft, to pagan magic rituals. We were linking up with some pretty cosmic things. It wasn't like 'Yeah, now we're all going to hold hands.' Fuck, the music just made you do it. Well, the drugs too.[8]

Walker conveys, in part, the inability to articulate the politics, the political part of a pleasure-political collective identity, because it is a moment that has to be lived. He, like all too many people involved in raving, resorts to mysticism, because what he is trying to convey is a mystery that can be experienced but not told. Of course, the inarticulate core of such a collective identity can be surrounded, prodded and even overwhelmed by attempts to explain it. The compulsion among some who are committed to such a politics to make people understand what is 'really' going on can be overwhelming. As one DJ noted of another DJ in the burgeoning rave scene in early 1990s Florida:

Kimball used to come and see me. He was always like, 'Oh you gotta come downtown, you have to see this club I do at the Beecham.' Finally, one night I went and I thought 'Wow, this is a great idea!' A big room, kinda dirty and all the music Kimball was playing and the Ecstasy . . . It was magic. Kimball was like 'I told you.'[9]

'I told you' could be the slogan of pleasure-politics; it conveys the certainty that when others feel as you do, they *will* understand that the world is different, can be different and should be different. Though I have focused on rave, with its combinations of drugs, spectacle and, above all, a constantly recreated collective body, the necessary incoherence of pleasure extends to other movements, such as those based around new, experimental or previously repressed sexualities.

A collective identity based on a pure form of affection and pleasure, which it is difficult, if not impossible, to communicate in any way other than by experiencing it, is the first axis of pleasure-politics. By reaching 'I told you', we can also perceive a second axis of activism!'s pleasure-politics in its necessary, collective solipsism. By collective solipsism, I mean the inability of individuals, all of them, to articulate what their collective identity is based on. It is the 'I told you' that can never be told.

Pleasure-politics is based on some form of shared experience and only becomes real within that experience. It creates one extreme form of collective identity in an identity whose truth can never be spoken, an identity that can only be experienced. The experience is all and the articulation nothing. Mary Anna Wright interviewed a number of Ecstasy users involved in rave culture and reported that many felt they had been 'let in on the biggest secret on earth' by taking E.[10] Here is one person's attempt to describe their rave experience:

> I just lost all track of time basically and I was just dancing all night . . . It was when people got into hugging everyone ridiculously and so you felt like everybody was your mate . . . You knew that everyone around was dancing away and into the same things but you were in your own little world. I got tapped on the shoulder once and I turned around and it was a 10-foot spaceman up on stilts with flashing lights waving at me and I went 'All right mate?' and he sort of stuck his thumbs up and started doing some mad dancing. It was quite surreal but it didn't freak me in any way: I just thought, 'Nice one'.[11]

Nice one, indeed. That 'nice one' is an expression of what the spaceman and the clubber know, but what the clubber cannot express except by pointing out details that only others who have similar experiences might understand. Necessary, collective solipsism is a collective identity that cannot be understood from outside. The only knowledge available that understands this collective identity is the knowledge that the identity has of itself. In the end, pleasure-politics is a radically self-defined politics.

It should be kept in mind that the identity in question is not that of an individual, but that of a collective created from many exchanges between texts, events, emotions, ideas and experiences. Such an understanding allows the integration into this theory of activism! of an insight expressed by Freud, Foucault and psychoanalytical practitioners, that we are not necessarily unified, organized subjects, but are fragmented selves that are constructed and reconstructed through the forces of unconscious, conscious and institutional interventions to regulate the self. This means that the construction of this collective solipsism allows for the fragmentation of people's individual identities. Pleasure-politics activist!s can experience the euphoria of a pleasure-political event on the weekend and return to work on the Monday, perhaps a little tired and with rings under their eyes, but nonetheless at work, conforming to a regulated self useful to state and corporation. Much criticism of pleasure-politics comes from this foregrounding of the fragmented self, because it allows people to separate or split their lived identities into a pleasure subject and a 'normal', or corporate/state, subject. While some individuals may need some form of splitting to give them a chance of understanding the powerful, necessarily inarticulate emotions pleasure-politics can produce, there are also processes of reconciliation when the contradictions between identities become too great. One example of this comes from the club Shoom, run by the Ramplings in the early stages of rave. One clubber . . .

> left her Filofax in a cab one night, with all her work contacts in it, she found herself wondering if it wasn't a sign that she should quite her job in PR and give herself up to the feeling completely. So many others felt the same that at one point the Ramplings had

to add a note in the hand-written newsletter they sent out to members pleading with them not to give up their day jobs.[12]

To give up your day job or not to give up your day job is a question posed often within pleasure-politics. This leads us from discussing the collective solipsism of a pleasure-politics in full swing to its final component: the transformation from solipsism to resistance. Although the left has often sniffed at pleasure-based movements, the right has not. The articulation of a pleasure-politics as political often comes from repression, and repression often comes from right and center-right moral crusades that take cultural politics seriously. The famous 'just say no' (to drugs) campaign and the infamous attempt by the Thatcher government to ban certain types of music ('those characterized by repetitive beats' is what it says in the legislation) are examples of what happens when right-wing politics suspect that something culturally transformative is occurring and tries to re-subject its subjects. Such a re-subjection necessarily cancels the core identity that pleasure-politicians embrace, thereby ruling out both the tactic of splitting to manage one's life and that of going fully revolutionary. If the core identity can be eliminated, then the pleasure-politics disappears altogether.

Under such an attack, a pleasure-politics may do a number of things. First, it can end and become a memory. The collective identity disappears when no selves are, any longer, performing it. This is usually the aim of repression, but it often fails because the experience fuelling the identity is too powerful for people to simply let it lapse. It also appears to those being re-subjected as an extraordinary injustice; they are, after all, engaging in pleasures that may appear to them to have no wider social consequences. Further, whatever the mainly state-based defenders of morality wish to happen, they can be contradicted by their corporate counterparts for whom a new pleasure can induce a feeding-frenzy of profit-making.

Second, pleasures can disappear from state view; they can continue underground, unseen, hidden. Games of cat and mouse can be played with a pleasure seeking its expression outside the gaze of regulating morality. Private spaces may be created, such as those sado-masochists have long inhabited, or those that ravers around the world created when their local police forces began paying too much attention to them. Whether such a tactic is successful or not depends on the repressing forces. If those seeking repression are willing to let a pleasure-politics continue because it is no longer public, or if the secrecy is successful and the pleasures are really thought to have disappeared, then this tactic may work. However, if the repression is too willing or if the secrecy is flawed, then repression will continue, leaving only two choices: to dissipate, rather than disappear, or to become political.

Third, pleasure can be articulated as a self-conscious politics. A public, political movement may begin with the aim of claiming the right to its collective identity. We do not need to dwell on this here, but only to imagine in passing how pleasure-politics have also, at times, become activism!s: pleasures of the body in gay, lesbian, bisexual and transgender movements; pleasure of the party and spirit in rave's connections to eco-activism; pleasures of the self in the women's movement's recreation of women's subjectivity; and so on.

Pleasure-politics is made out of these three axes: meaning as emotion, collective solipsism and the reaction to repression. Strung across a field constructed by these three poles is a pleasure-politics that contributes to activism! both for its own political effects and in its connections to other elements.

The De-Radicalization of Pleasure

Pleasure-politics, of all the themes of activism!, is the one that stands on a knife-edge. On the one side is the transgression of cultural norms that means pleasure-politics is part of activism! and produces new symbols, pleasures and bodies. On the other side is an easy drift into solipsism and mysticism along a self-defeating path of self-definition. Before moving on from pleasure-politics we should touch on these failures and recognize that they are a possibility always present when pleasure is a transgression.

Solipsism is essential to pleasure-politics; it is its very inability to articulate what is occurring that makes it such a powerful and transformative experience. However, this can lead in several directions. In addition to culturally engaged forms of pleasure-politics, solipsism can lead into a self-regarding detachment from any social or cultural base. Instead of transgressing cultural norms, a pleasure-politics can begin to ascribe its experiences to asocial means, often as a way of explaining the all-powerful experience. Here, biological, mystical and chemical means may begin to be venerated as sources of social change, effectively detaching a pleasure-politics from its politics. This can be seen in the dance cultures that have formed the key example of this chapter:

Ecstasy seems to make people more determined to cooperate with one another. One reason for this is a physical response to the chemical's action in the brain. The subtle changes in behaviour caused by Ecstasy have brought about a revolution . . . The action of MDMA on the brain is to cause the release of seratonin and dopamine. These chemicals are neurotransmitters which alter the messages passed between brain cells and so affect mood. The result is that Ecstasy produces a similar feeling to being in love, and can induce feelings of empathy.[13]

It is not unusual for the drug of choice of a particular movement to have nearly magical powers ascribed to it; here, greater feelings of social solidarity are put down to chemicals. We need only think of the effects LSD was supposed to have created in the late 1960s, or the importance of amphetamines to the mid–late-1970s punk movement, to see other instances in which drugs have been thought to change society. Such under-standings remove social content; they ignore political, cultural and economic factors to find non-human interventions that explain the all-powerful emotional experience pleasure-politics can produce. A second example of a non-social agency that often emerges is mystical beliefs. Pagan spirituality has been an important influence on much modern eco-activist and animal-liberation thought. At times, though, this also shifts from a socially engaged spirituality into a socially disengaged spirituality, in which the politics of pleasure is ascribed to gods and spirits beyond the human world. This process, at its most alarming, can result in a reverse racism that venerates non-Western cultures:

> the imagery invoked by many . . . of rave as hypnotic, tribal, even primal, carries dangerous suppositions of western supremacy over a caricatured valorisation of savages in grass skirts banging tom-tom drums, and is deeply offensive to those of contemporary tribal communities.[14]

A self-defined politics that cannot be articulated has the potential to become a self-righteously solipsistic politics. It can be a politics of activists talking only to each other and convinced that only they understand what only the converted truly know. The danger of pleasure-politics is that plea-sure leads away from cultures and not towards transgression of them.

'It's like a jungle some times, makes me wonder . . .'

Activist! pleasure-politics transgresses codes and cultures of behaviour and, in doing so, transgresses the ways selves, personalities and subjects are created and maintained. It does so by creating an extreme collective identity in which common experience can barely be named let alone described. These are movements in which feelings, the highs and lows, the emotions, are completely in themselves the meaning of the movement. This creates a collective solipsism in that only someone who chooses to transgress and to taste the experience can become part of the movement and engage with pleasure-based collective identities. By definition, they will only be able to express their understanding of their transgression through a nod of recognition with others who are similarly experienced. Though politicized by their transgression of current, socially normal means of regulating selves, pleasure-political movements commonly become consciously politicized when their pleasures are repressed. The threat to the regulation of all selves is sometimes perceived to be so great that repressive forces engage with private pleasures: the criminalization of music, the outlawing of parties, the prosecution of consensual sexual acts and, perhaps above all, the demonization of some drugs.

Pleasure is most commonly thought of as an adjunct to protest, a vehicle through which a group might express and progress its politics. I have not analyzed this connection of pleasure and politics closely here because these uses of pleasures are discussed elsewhere in this book. Mediated through many experiences, however, it is possible for a pleasure to become the core of a collective identity that draws disorganized selves together into transgression. Such transgressions can be serious enough to be identified and attacked. When pleasure is politics, it may become a state crime.

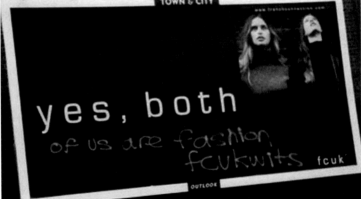

CHAPTER FIVE

Culture Jamming and Semiotic Terrorism

Reality isn't what it used to be.
Mark Dery [1]

Symbolic Codes

One day, someone who shared my politics bought a bumper sticker for the Australian Labour Party. It was election time, and the sticker said 'EMPLOY LABOUR NOW'. I was shocked. The Labour Party was, we then thought, a contemptible reformist organization. My acquaintance was sheepish, as though he knew that he was being naughty. We went back to his office; with the snip of some scissors, he now had a sticker that was indistinguishable from all of the other red-and-white stickers imploring us to employ Labour, expect that my friend's now read 'NO LABOUR PLOY'. Culture jam.

A television advertisement starts as slickly as any other. It first shows a car with the portentous voice-over 'It's coming . . . The most significant

101

event in automotive history.' So far, so normal. The car moves further into view, revealing itself to be part of the arm of some sort of creature. The creature moves further and further into shot, appearing as a huge monster made out of cars that is smashing and destroying the earth around it. The voice-over continues. 'It's coming . . . The end of the age of the automobile. Imagine: a world with less cars.' You gradually realize that this advert is attacking car use by claiming that car use is destroying the planet. By the end, instead of half-watching, you find yourself paying close attention, trying to work out whether the message really is what you think it is and looking to see who made the advert. You have seen millions of adverts urging you to buy a car, but never one urging you to abandon cars. This disjunction between familiar advertising techniques and unfamiliar message means culture jam.[2]

Each of these examples of culture jamming is an attempt to reverse and transgress the meaning of cultural codes whose primary aim is to persuade us to buy something or be someone. The first is an intervention against techniques to sell a political party, the second an intervention against techniques to sell us a lifestyle based on the car. Both are more than simple anti-advertising actions, because the cultural codes they contest stretch from pressuring us to buy a certain product to formulating collective desires and needs. These cultural codes of purchasing are owned and controlled by corporations and states who fund them to extraordinarily high levels. The aim of these codes is to generate ways of life, forms of identity and human needs that serve their funders. Such attempts to form the lives of all of us in ways that meet not our needs, however we manage to define those, but the needs of, on the one hand, corporations whose ultimate goal is a profitable bottom line and, on the other hand, states whose ultimate aim is to manage its citizens, can be resisted. The codes can be jammed. The cultures that are foisted on us, coming not from communities or individuals or families, but from profit-seeking companies and their hired semioticians, can be turned inside out. There are the hired symbol makers of advertising and public relations and the wired semiotic terrorists of culture jamming.

When major, almost inescapable, cultural codes have been colonized by some sectors of society and turned to their needs, through the massive creative resources that corporate and state funding can command, then activism! finds itself resisting through symbols. These corporate and state cultural codes have come to dominate and constitute much of the landscapes of our desires, explicitly and all too successfully recreating and moulding our passions to their needs. The language of corporate desire is a language too many of us speak fluently and unthinkingly. Culture jammers begin from this vision of cultural disaster and turn the languages against themselves. Out of this confrontation they hope both to disrupt the subordination of our needs to the needs of profit and to open up new languages through which desires and needs may be defined by individuals and communities. The beginning point of culture jamming is the already existing and dominant cultural codes that permeate our languages of desire and personal need. The end point of culture jamming is hoped to be a smoking ruin of corporate and state codes and as yet unimagined ways of generating desires.

To understand the ambiguities, powers and faults of culture jamming, we need to pass through three related aspects of it. First, we need to sketch in the basic techniques of semiotic terrorism. We need to see symbols being contested. Second, we need to extend this sketch into the more complex arena of cultural codes, particularly by taking up branding. Finally, we need to explore the great danger of culture jamming in that it is constantly being recuperated. All of activism! faces this problem, the drawing of activism!'s teeth by incorporating it into deradicalized social change, but only culture jamming has recuperation as a central, constituent possibility. Semiotic terrorism, codes and recuperation are the three key axes or dimensions of culture jamming.

Semiotic Terrorism

Semiotic terrorism refers to individual acts of culture jamming. By calling it semiotic, I refer to the entirely symbolic terrain of struggle. Acts of culture jamming exist within systems of symbols. The field of semiotics is a complex one, with detailed theoretical and empirical analyses of the way in which signs function and what they mean. Such complex thinking is not absent from culture jamming, but it is tempered by the immediate demands of political activity. It is not necessary here to divert suddenly into a complex definition of what 'semiotic' means, simply to note that within activism! it means both individual symbols, such as a picture on a billboard, and the codes of signification that individual symbols are part of, such as various conventions for producing and viewing advertisements. It is the aim of culture jamming to terrorize the symbols and codes that make up the semiotics that subordinate our desires to corporate and state imperatives. This is bloodless terror, as it is the symbols that are terrorized, not the semioticians (excluding the odd custard pie wielded in the name of liberation). Semiotic terrorism contests the meanings of our world. The power of an effective moment of semiotic terrorism is based on using the same language as that being criticized. The power of transforming 'EMPLOY LABOUR NOW' into 'NO LABOUR PLOY!' was that the two bumper stickers had the same 'look and feel'. The Labour sticker used certain colours and a font that the jammed sticker also used, meaning that people familiar with one political slogan were jolted by the unfamiliar meaning clothed in the familiar style. A good act of semiotic terrorism works on these two levels. First, it directly undermines a particular target. Second, the languages through which messages are sold to us, the public, are brought out of their normal, assumed status and made explicit. Once a disjunction occurs between the message and the medium, the medium itself becomes an object for discussion.

We can see how this works in practice. In October 1978, in San

Francisco, a billboard advertising cigarettes featured a half-naked, moustached man (referred to as The Turk) with a beautiful woman at his shoulder looking admiringly at him. He was, of course, smoking a cigarette. As the culture jammers said of him 'The Turk was very 70's: macho, bare chested, steely gaze; a veritable disco inferno.'[3] Culture jammers, in this case the Billboard Liberation Front (BLF), dressed the macho man in a nice pink bra.[4] In the culture-jammed version, the accompanying 'One of a kind' finally seemed appropriate. Such activities require thought, planning and a willingness to transgress some laws. Here is the BLF's version of this culture jam:

> This improvement was the idea of our old PR guy Simon Wagstaff. There was a Camel board across from his flat & he had to stare at the Turk each day over his morning coffee. He felt we needed to point out the fact that most of us fellas that smoked weren't quite so macho. We might cough when we smoked . . . The BLF mobilized . . . As with all of our meticulously plotted and surgically executed operations we intended to cover the entire outdoor advertising landscape with our 'new', 'improved' Ad image. We succeeded in installing three bras . . . at three different locations. At the third location, Simon kicked the bucket. The bucket of RUBBER CEMENT. It happened while we were diving onto the plank just below the recently bra'd Turk. We were hiding from the SFPD [San Francisco Police Department] cruiser that had pulled into the parking lot & parked almost directly beneath us. The officer sat there, 20 feet below us doing his paperwork while a light breeze steadily pushed the acrid odor of dripping rubber cement away from his open window. We held position for over an hour not moving a muscle. Later we tracked rubber cement into a local drinking establishment.[5]

In this action, the language of advertisement was uncovered through the fracturing of the macho man's sexuality. The enticement to gain desirable sexual partners by buying certain products was uncovered as a trick of the ad-man's trade. Both the content and language of this billboard were brought into question.

Though cigarette companies are a favourite target of billboard jammers such as the BLF and Buga-Up (Billboard Utilising Graffiti Against Unhealthy Products), their culture jamming is focused on the fact of adverts rather than particular products. This can be seen in another BLF action from April 2001. Fortune magazine had created a billboard featuring Jeff Bezos's face with the slogan 'In the land of the blind, the one-eyed man is king.' Bezos is Chief Executive Officer of Amazon.com, one of the major e-commerce sites that sprang up during the late 1990s. This billboard was a challenge to the then major downturn in high-technology stocks, because it proclaimed Bezos's commitment to building the profile of his company, rather than turning a profit with it (something he had failed to do), as the wisdom of the one-eyed man. This, in turn, promoted the magazine as the place where you would find the wisdom of the one-eyed man, which would help you profit in the market-place. The BLF placed two large pennies over Bezos's eyes to symbolize his death. They also altered the slogan to read 'In the land of the dead, the one-eyed man is king.' Here, again, both the advertiser's content and language were questioned. The advice to invest in high-tech stocks, from magazines like Fortune, had, by 2001, landed many small American investors in debt, because many of those stocks had become worthless or, in financial terms, had died. This was not the message Fortune wanted, but the one the BLF produced. The language of the billboard that originally attempted to create meaning somewhere between the slogan and the picture of Bezos was uncovered through its radical revision. The BLF had earlier conducted a similar jam on a wide range of billboards advertising Internet companies by adding a sticker produced to look like a computer-error message which stated 'Fatal Error: Invalid Stock Value'.[6]

Another series of examples can be found in Adbusters, a magazine and culture-jamming network. The magazine follows culture jams and corporations, reporting on events and analyzing the struggle to transgress corporate codes. It records culture jams, for example, in a series of spoof ads. There is a picture of Ronald McDonald, with the word Grease (the two 'e's are the Golden Arches symbol on their side) written into his red lipstick. Absolut vodka has sponsored a series of advertisements that feature the word Absolut and another word indicating the attraction of the drink (such as Fun). Adverts that look to have come from exactly the same series can be found on Adbusters with slogans such as 'Absolut Impotence', featuring a picture of a flaccid, bending vodka bottle, or 'Absolut End', featuring an outline of a bottle drawn on the ground like that of a dead body at a crime scene. Another alcoholic-beverage company, Smirnoff, has a series of adverts featuring repeated images, one of which is altered by being seen through the bottle. For example, a series of bored-looking party guests are interrupted by the wild-looking party seen through the bottle. Adbusters have turned this company into Smirkoff in an advert featuring laughing children, except for the one seen through the bottle who has been battered. A spoof of Calvin Klein adverts for its fragrance 'Obsession' has already been mentioned. In a second version, the slogan 'Obsession for Women' is placed over the back of a naked, lithe woman who can be made out clutching her stomach and leaning over a toilet bowl, vomiting to maintain her advertiser-defined body.[7]

In each Adbuster spoof, care is taken to make the advert appear as close as possible to the original. These advertising series are thus turned against their original intention as the meaning of the adverts is undermined; a fragrance is unmasked as male narcissism and female self-damage; a bottle of vodka is presented as threatening to life. In each case, the language of the original adverts is faithfully reproduced, meaning that the language itself becomes a topic. The attempt of advertisers to have us associate a perfect body with a fragrance, or fun and virility with an alcoholic drink, is made obvious by using the language of advertisers to produce opposed associations. Adbusters, like all culture jammers, aims simultaneously at each advert and at the cultural codes defining our desires in ways that serve corporations and not individuals or communities.

There are many more such moments of semiotic terrorism:[8] bumper stickers that state 'I'm changing the climate, ask me how' are attached to gas-guzzling, environment-threatening cars; a rubber stamp stating 'We are sorry, a rubber stamp has been affixed to your letter' is stamped on a letter just where a rubber-stamped advert might appear; an advert for a Canadian lottery has its slogan replaced by one that states 'Winning; only 14 times harder than guessing someone's P.I.N. number'; the slogan on a MacDonald's billboard reading 'Feeling hungry all of a sudden?' becomes 'Feeling heavy all of a sudden?'; and, on a busy street, someone places sods of grass in a parking place with chairs and a cool drink. The question is, of course, what overall justifications make these acts more than isolated moments of humour and anger? Is culture jamming about something systemic or something fleeting?

It's the Brand, Stupid . . . Or Informational Capitalism

Branding is the key to culture jamming in its broadest political sense. This is not because branding is the only enemy attacked by culture jamming, but because examining branding is the most direct way of identifying what it is that culture jammers are for and against. Branding connects semiotic terrorism to the general corporate and state cultural codes that are the ultimate targets of culture jamming.

Branding refers to a type of advertising strategy that attempts to sell an image, approach or lifestyle rather than a product. The most famous branding has been that of Nike, whose particular symbol, the 'swoosh' as it is called, can be seen almost everywhere, from the ear of Australia's most famous active cricketer to the baseball caps worn by millions. Nike sells not so much the quality of its shoes, clothes, caps or whatever else it puts its brand on, as the brand itself. For example, the company hires famous people, especially sports personalities, and then designs campaigns that hardly talk about the product, instead seducing the consumer into the dream of being like Michael Jordan or Tiger Woods. As one Nike campaign exhorted, 'be like Mike.' At a second, often barely conscious, level, Nike tries to invade our deepest, unthought desires with images of how wonderful life can be when the swoosh is on it: people on wild cycling trips, people playing ecstatic basketball, perfect bodies running to their 'limit'. All these and more are images within the Nike world. Taken together, what Nike, and all other brand-builders, seek to achieve is consumer recognition integrated with consumer approval. The Nike website for women is called NikeGoddess; if you buy Nike, you don't get shoes, you get to be a goddess.

This approach to advertising refuses to preach the virtues of a product directly, instead looking for the long-term benefits of being able to sell anything that a symbol can be placed on because that symbol meets deeply held desires. It is this corporate production of symbolic codes, which attempts to structure our unconscious desires and needs, that is most deeply opposed by culture jammers. Branding is key, because it shows most clearly where and why culture jamming confronts certain ways of seeing, feeling and hearing.

Culture jamming, however obsessed with advertising it can be, does not stop with corporate branding. Dery has argued that what can be called an Empire of Signs has emerged:

In America, factory capitalism has been superseded by an information economy characterized by the reduction of labor to the manipulation, on computers, of symbols that stand for the production process. The engines of industrial production have slowed, yielding to a phantasmagoric capitalism that produces intangible commodities – Hollywood blockbusters, television sitcoms, catchphrases, jingles, buzzwords, images, one-minute megatrends, financial transactions flickering through fiberoptic bundles. Our wars are Nintendo wars, fought with camera-equipped smart bombs that marry cinema and weaponry in a television that kills.[9]

Dery connects branding's corporate cultural codes, codes that offer seduction in return for consumption, to wider cultural codes through which our worlds are constructed. The Gulf War of 1990–91 is often called the Nintendo war, because it was played out before often horrified, sometimes exulted world audiences through images generated on the battlefield. These were images that looked as if they had come straight from the latest video game. We have since seen many such images, but it is hard to underestimate the impact of these first instances when the world viewed pictures taken from a bomb as it fell towards its target, or from the plane or helicopter that launched the weapon. The video-game-like nature of these images both engaged audiences, as if the war were their own and they were implicated in the pulled trigger, and trivialized loss of life. The cultural analyst Baudrillard went so far as to argue that, in his famous phrase, 'the Gulf War did not take place', and was, rather, a media event. The positive sense that can be made of Baudrillard's claim is not that blood was not shed, especially as Iraqi casualties are likely to have been over a hundred thousand while Allied casualties were under three hundred, but that the war we saw and the war that was fought were different things. The war did not take place for all those watching; instead, a simulation of it was played out, tailored to the needs of the military and the dominant nation-states. The military branded the Gulf War.

We can make this process concrete if we touch on controls on the press exercised by the US and allied military during the Gulf War. All reporters covering the American and allied armies had to be accompanied by military escorts during interviews. All reporting was done collectively, which meant that small groups of reporters produced news shared by all. This process led to control over both content and reporting speed. One in ten reports by journalists about the fast-moving 'ground war' took longer than three days to reach their news organizations, longer than during the American Civil War. As Colin Powell, then head of the US military, said, 'Once you've got all the forces moving and everything's being taken care of . . . turn your attention to television. Because you can win the battle [but] lose the war if you don't handle your story right.'[10] Handling your story right means ensuring that the stories that come back from the front reflect the 'right' agenda. Generals exhort other generals to brand their wars.

In these ways, even amid the so-called chaos of war, participants seek control of meaning. Ways of ensuring that even the bloodiest military actions can enter homes as broad cultural codes are created and exploited. Dery's Empire of Signs permeates our lives in more ways than advertising. Having just touched on its military values, we can imagine other ways in which those who can afford to buy cultural professionals will seek to produce cultural codes defining desires and needs that benefit their narrow interests. I need only mention the vast sums paid by political parties for polling, advertisements, focus groups, spin doctors and the like, to open up cultural codes of politics.

It is against all of these codes that culture jamming takes aim and within which jammers frolic. For example, the projects of sometime culture jammers RTMark, undertaken since 1993, include jams against the World Trade Organization and neo-liberalism (Yesmen), moral panics (Y2K panic), gender roles (Barbie), video games and sexualities (Simcopter), work (Phone in Sick Day), online rights (Etoy campaign) and political campaigns (Presidential Exploratory Committee).[11] Jammers will find transgression wherever symbols and signs are systematized into a cultural code for the benefit of a small group. Wherever acts of semiotic terrorism can be waged, culture jammers will be able to unpick the message, the language and the code that lie within.

Recuperation: The Endless Game of Signs

The strategy of playing diversity, itineracy, uniqueness in time, against universal laws and an engineered social order is no longer enough, because conditions have changed. Unlike the authoritarian state, globalized capitialism does not seek control of desire, but control through desire, the channeling of experience and otherness in cycles of consumption and (increasingly symbolic) production. It seeks a kind of open, inventive, productive compliance . . . Under this new regime, each space of freedom you create is potentially open to colonization, manipulation. Disruptive gestures are not prohibited but studied, emulated.[12]

A series of billboard advertisements appeared in Australia in 2000 for a new football boot made by Nike. This occurred in the context of several years of organized protest against Nike's use of sweatshop – even slave and prison – labour to produce the material commodities to which it attached its brand. The slogan on these adverts was 'The most offensive boots we've ever made'. Of course, the word offence relates closely to sport, in which being offensive may have other connotations than Nike's labour practices. Yet it is possible to detect a strange, tongue-in-cheek nod to their opponents here. The next stage of the campaign was for Nike to jam their own billboards. Just as culture jammers and billboard liberators paste over offensive adverts, Nike had new messages pasted over their slogan: 'What next, rocket packs?' and 'Fair-Minded Footy Fans say Not Fair Mr Technology'. The group Fair-Minded Footy Fans (FMFF) had their own website on which they made it plain that they were protesting against the superlative Nike boots, which made the game unfair on those who did not wear them. Of course, FMFF was a product of Nike advertising and not, at all, a grass-roots campaign to make football fairer. Culture jamming had been incorporated into advertising as one more technique. The corporate code had swallowed its opposition.

Culture jammers were not impressed; they would prefer to be indigestible. Soon, a further slogan was being plastered underneath the offensively tinged original and not over it. The billboard now read: 'The most offensive boot we've ever made. 100% slave labour.' The backlash against Nike's campaign saw the company receiving publicity they could not have gotten from any 'normal' ad campaign and then agreeing to drop the campaign altogether. There were yet further layers within. Towards the end of a retelling of this story on one highly critical website appeared a statement that '. . . this text was supposed to have been found on a photocopied poster stuck on a Melbourne Nike billboard, and was emailed to us.' Just before this note, which was the first hint that this website might not be what it seemed, were the final paragraphs of this found text:

BUT THE MOST SCARY FACT OF ALL IS THIS: Nike has commissioned me to write and distribute this article. They paid me a very handsome sum up front and further bonuses according to any media coverage it gets. This includes the number of times this text passes around email networks, something Nike considers a crucial form of information distribution . . . You may be disappointed in me. You may wonder how such a seemingly intelligent and moral voice like mine could possibly shake hands with the devil. I do this as a photo opportunity for you to ponder, a cultural soundbyte for you to ruminate upon. Nike not only fucks with the lives of innocent people in developing countries, it also deeply fucks with our emotions in rich countries. How could you never name the demon that possesses Western culture? Our protest over the mistreatment of overseas workers is largely emotional projection. What we really need to focus on is the cultural violation it does to us every time we are bombarded with their imagery. You need to discern the receding horizon of cultural reality for yourselves; you can't rely on people like me to show it to you. What are the implications of Nike owning the cultural critique of itself? REALLY THINK ABOUT IT. Unfortunately I can't fight this battle because I am not real. I was created by corporate funding.[13]

The complexity was now entirely unnerving. Was this a site put up by Nike, by someone paid by Nike, or by someone opposed to Nike quoting a text found on a poster? Could Nike really pay for a website laden with links to some of its most powerful critics? Had a jammer taken money to teach other jammers a lesson? It was almost impossible to discern from examining the website or its links what was going on. What was most undermining for culture jamming is that the anonymous demand to really think about Nike owning its own cultural critique strikes home. Is culture jamming failing because even in its very acts of semiotic terrorism it reinforces the cultural codes that call for these acts in the first place? Does the use of corporate, military or state cultural codes reinforce these codes, even when the overt message is to oppose them?

A second example may help. In mid-2001, a number of stencils appeared on walls in London. These were of someone looking obviously like a Zapatista guerrilla (balaclava, military garb, bandolier) and possibly like Subcomandante Marcos (the pipe was smudged, but possibly there) with the slogan underneath 'We are you.' Pro-Zapatista jamming of urban walls, perhaps? But no. A British clothes company, Box Fresh, specializing in 'urbanware' had produced a line of clothing and was advertising it using both images and words from the Zapatistas. The Box Fresh shop was adorned with Zapatista pictures and had Marcos's words printed on walls and windows. Culture-jamming techniques had been incorporated into advertising again, and, again, there was a response. Alongside the stencils of Marcos with the slogan 'We are you' appeared new words: 'No you're not, you're an overpriced shop trying to be subversive. Box Fresh makes me ill' and, in a bubble coming from Marcos's mouth, 'Don't shop at Box Fresh, they're trying to turn the Zapatistas into an advert.' Alongside these responses, less semiotic tactics emerged. Activists wearing balaclavas leafleted the shop, and an email and letter writing campaign began.

The culture jammers who instigated this campaign, a group called space hijackers, then reported that Box Fresh's head of advertising, the advert designer and the company's owner called a meeting at which they reported being told that Box Fresh were not a 'bunch of nasties'. Box Fresh, they reported, stated that 'You caught us with our pants down, and we realize we were wrong' and agreed to four conditions. They would donate every penny of profit from their Zapatista merchandise to the Zapatistas themselves. They would install a computer in the shop with a range of Zapatista sites on it. They would no longer put their logo on the adverts with Subcomandante Marcos's words on them. And they would have a leaflet in the store explaining the history of the Zapatistas and, in all further marketing, attempt to spread information about the Zapatista cause and their ethics as opposed to simply using them in soundbites and as an aesthetic.[14] As the spacehijackers admitted, they would have preferred the clothing to have been withdrawn, but they were 'bloody surprised to have even got this far'. Unless, of course, the spacehijackers were themselves part of Box Fresh's plans? What if spacehijackers were generating publicity for Box Fresh? What if the aim was to gain free publicity by becoming a news story?

The point of this story is that the cynicism that implies that all reports of culture jamming must be treated with scepticism in case the 'enemy' is the real author is inherent within culture jamming. The potential for recuperation is invited by the decision to use the enemies' language to subvert the enemy.

Is There an Outside to the Empire of Signs?

Perhaps recuperation is a reason for abandoning and rejecting culture jamming. Certainly, there has been criticism of it from within activism!. For example, the look of the Adbusters magazine is glossy, like the magazines it is criticizing, so it is hard to tell them apart at first glance. Such confusions are also the point of culture jamming. Any rejection of culture jamming because of recuperation presumes that there is a way outside the Empire of Signs created by corporations and states. For culture jamming to be rejected in principle, there must be the possibility that a language can exist not dependent on or engaged with dominant cultural codes. Certainly, culture jammers see the necessity of languages free of corporate and state codes. The ultimate aim of culture jamming, in as much as it has one aim, must be to develop languages that articulate needs and desires generated by individuals and communities in dialogue with each other, rather than through codes determined by state or corporate needs. But if there were needs and desires already existing pure and untouched by corporate or state cultural codes, then culture jamming might be wrong. It could be argued that nurturing pure cultural codes would be far more transgressive than engaging with already poisoned codes. Is there an outside to the Empire of Signs? If there is, then culture jamming is playing in the wrong semiotic sandbox.

A pillar of culture jamming is revealed in the answer 'No, culture jammers believe there is no outside to the Empire of Signs.' There are no arenas of life that the state or corporations (or both) do not touch. There is no purity unaffected by dominant cultural practices. Nothing is free from these codes, from the most intimate moments of sexual life (think of Aids campaigns by the state or the sexualization of advertising by corporations) or family life (think of government advice or images of what a happy family should be in corporate eyes) or sport, or nature, or children's imaginations or any other aspect of human life that can be thought of. Everywhere, we find information, images, norms and needs generated, defined and managed through cultural codes produced by the professionals of desire. Culture jamming's hope cannot be that something pure exists in a media-saturated world. Rather, it hopes that needs different to those that are currently dominant can be generated from our current world. Culture jamming works inside the Empire of Signs to create an outside, to open breaches through which needs undefined by profit or bureaucratic logic can be generated and regenerated. Culture jamming begins from the pessimism that cultural codes and languages of desire already exist and are already dominated by profit and state rationalities.

Yet culture jamming will never be unambiguous. It will always remain an open question whether its attempt to work with the tools of its enemy fundamentally compromises it as a political tactic. Even accepting that there is no simple alternative to the languages of corporate and state desire, it remains unclear whether culture jamming offers a way beyond these languages or is potentially another version of them. We might even speculate that this tension fuels some of the creativity of culture jamming, that the constant flirting with the enemy also generates some of its excitement. However successful a jam or some jammers may be, the spectre of recuperation will never be completely banished from the politics of culture jamming. By taking up these languages and subverting them, culture jamming risks making the Empire of Signs even more impregnable. Just as in all activism!, hope and risk run side by side.

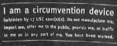

I am a circumvention device

forbidden by 17 USC 1201(a)(3). Do not manufacture me,
import me, offer me to the public, provide me, or traffic
in me or in any part of me. You have been warned.

CHAPTER SIX

Hacktivism: All Together in the Virtual

Hacking, Cracking, Activism and Hacktivism

Hacktivism is politically motivated hacking. Hacktivism is activism! running free in the electronic veins that enliven our 21st-century, global socio-economies.

So many of us now spend time staring at computer screens. Imagine using a networked screen for work or leisure, and it suddenly ceases to function. You try to input commands, but nothing happens. Suddenly, your screen reads 'All files are being deleted. All files are being deleted.' The same thing is happening to everyone else's computer. The message scrolls and scrolls, and there is nothing anyone can do to prevent it – that is, until someone takes emergency action and pulls electric plugs from their sockets, killing the disaster in the crudest way. These actions were played out in 1988 at the National Aeronautical and Space Administration (NASA) in America. Someone had planted a program on their network that continually copied itself to any other computer connected to the NASA network. These files continued to replicate until each computer ceased to function. The message that files were being deleted turned out to be false, a provocation. The program had been planted by someone protesting against NASA launching space probes that included small nuclear reactors, often described by protesters as potential nuclear bombs. This was hacktivism before the term was invented.

Hacking has occurred since computer networks emerged. Originally, a 'hack' referred to innovative uses of technology. One hacker used the following example: If you wanted a cup of tea and did not have an electric kettle, but did have a coffee maker and used it to heat the water for your tea, this unexpected use of a coffee maker was a hack. Since this initial formulation, hacking has become associated in the mass media with illicit computer intrusion rather than with innovative uses of technology. This has led to the definition of cracking, a term many hackers use to refer to unwanted entry into computer systems by explorers or criminals. Both of these senses of 'hacker' – that is, both hacker and cracker – are relevant to hacktivism, which involves the dis/organized eruption of non-cyberspatial politics in the hacking community. When the word *hacker* is used here, it should not be thought only to refer to people breaking into computer systems, but to all the possibile novel uses of technology.

In 1996, the Critical Arts Ensemble (CAE) issued a call for the development of electronic civil disobedience and the politicization of hackers. They argued that power was shifting from physical locations, embodied in slogans about 'power in the streets', to virtual locations. The élites, they argued, were increasingly making and remaking the world through electronic flows of power, through cyberspace. CAE called for the tactics of blockage and siege developed by civil disobedience to be reinvented in the virtual realm. They pointed out that power derives increasingly from cyberspatial information flows, and these flows can be blocked.[1] By 1998, these ideas had been turned into one kind of reality with the Electronic

Disturbance Theatre's (EDT) attempt to support the Zapatistas through online direct action. They launched a software tool called Floodnet that attempted to constantly reload a targeted website (often that of the Mexican President) in an attempt to slow it down by bombarding it with requests. Floodnet also automated the production of satirical messages from the targeted site. For example, someone targeting a computer would see messages reporting a failure to find a page on a site, with the automated message reading something like 'no human rights found on this server' or 'no democracy found on this server.'

Prior to the emergence of hacktivists like EDT, the politics of hacking was almost exclusively focused on virtual issues with an overriding ethic that held free flows of information, securely accessible to all, to be the highest principle. Hacker politics focused on issues such as the security of computer systems and the implications of security for the privacy of individuals. Such politics also concentrated on discovering ways around censorship of the Internet, often utilizing its global nature to undermine attempts by nation-states to censor content. For example, when the Italian hacktivist/activist website Netstrike was seized by magistrates in 2001, copies or mirrors of the Netstrike site were almost instantly set up around the world, thus evading Italy's national jurisdiction. As well as copies of the site, packages of files that allowed anyone to mirror the site were also made available, meaning that as one mirror might be closed, activists would have the means of creating another one. This example demonstrates a common hacker politics of using the Internet to create and maintain free flows of information.

The rise of hacktivism has not superseded or destroyed previous hacker politics, but has reconfigured it within a broader political landscape. This distinction between 'informational politics', traditionally the centre of hacker politics, and a broadening out into non-virtual politics is a useful one, as it separates out the two main streams of hacktivism. To fully explore these transgressions of the information infrastructures of 21st-century socio-economies, I will look at each of these hacktivist strands in turn.

MVDA: Mass Virtual Direct Action

Mass virtual direct action complicates and extends non-violent direct action. Taking notions of violence and action into cyberspace involves a shift of reality. Things are not the same online as they are offline, and the metaphors or analogies so often used to understand virtual life through real life are slippery. For example, hacking is often described as burglary or theft, and some of the descriptions I have given above imply something similar; hacking is illicit, it is intrusion, it cracks someone's computer. However, if a hacker is a thief, then s/he is the strangest of thieves, because no matter what is stolen, an exact copy is also left behind. Which real-world burglar both takes your video and leaves your video behind? This cannot happen, of course, and this distinction means that we should be wary of applying words to the electronic world that make sense when describing the physical one. With this cautionary statement in mind, we can look at some examples of MVDA and then explore each of its constituent parts.

During the World Trade Organization (WTO) meeting in Seattle in 1999, there were simultaneous online and offline protests. As demonstrators occupied the streets, hacktivists occupied websites. These protests were set up by a group called the Electrohippie Collective (or ehippies). The ehippies created a small software program that was embedded in a web-page. Anyone who chose to go to that web-page to participate in the protest would automatically download a copy of the program and begin using it from their computer. The program repeatedly loaded pages from the WTO network. If enough people went to the ehippies site, if enough computers were thus running the ehippies program, the WTO network would be overwhelmed with requests and brought to a halt. This virtual action was harmonized with the street actions whose aim was to halt the WTO conference. The attempt to physically prevent the conference from occurring was matched by an attempt to block information flows serving WTO delegates.

The ehippies claim that around 450,000 computers participated in the action over five days and that the WTO network was halted on two occasions and significantly slowed through much of the conference.[2]

The ehippies action against the WTO was, in some political ways, similar to EDT's Floodnet,[3] in that both targeted a particular website and attempted to make a point by flooding it with requests. However, EDT has not aimed to bring down a targeted website; instead, it has attempted to make a political protest by slowing a target and by ensuring that suddenly increased traffic on a site is clearly related to a political purpose. A later ehippies action used a similar model when protesting against the Free Trade Area of the Americas (FTAA) conference in Quebec in 2001. Rather than trying to bring down the targeted network, the ehippies attempted 'to demonstrate that online action could be constructed to make a point in a directed manner, rather than seeking to cause indiscriminate closure of a site'.[4]

Similar actions have been taken up by other groups with varying levels of technological sophistication. The Italian group Netstrike has the following advice: 'Now insert the target web address in your navigation bar. Keep clicking Reload continuously.'[5] Sitting at your computer repeatedly pressing the reload button may be boring, but it has a similar effect to utilizing software designed to do the same thing automatically (such software is also thoughtfully made available by Netstrike). Another low-tech MVDA was the 1999 Global Jam Echelon day. Echelon is a world-wide surveillance network run by the American government in conjunction with other governments, on whose land the US runs listening stations. It is believed that Echelon not only intercepts telecommunications traffic, but, where possible, subjects what it captures to keyword searches. The idea was that, on a single day, many people would send emails including 50 keywords most likely picked up by Echelon, including 'bomb', 'hacktivism', 'terrorist' and the like. The hope was that a sudden increase in suspicious emails would overload Echelon. While nobody on the 'outside' of the relevant security agencies might ever know the result, it was hoped that the combustion of the system would send a message to those on the 'inside'. The technological abilities here are as low as cyberspace can make them – choosing 50 words and sending an email. Other MVDA's have supported or targeted the G8 meeting in Genoa; the American military's use of Vieques for bombing practice; Lufthansa airline for its participation in the deportation of asylum seekers; the Harvard University living-wage campaign; Starbucks coffee shops; the death penalty in the state of Texas; and more. If we look at the various elements that make up MVDA, we can see how such actions begin to translate mass civil disobedience and street protest into protests that play in the electronic nervous system of 21st-century societies. We can divide these actions into three components: mass, virtual and direct action. In each case, it is essential to pay attention to the distinctions between real and virtual environments.

'Mass' means that these actions are meaningless unless a large number of people participate. This may seem obvious, but large numbers of people mean quite different things in cyberspace, where what 'people' can do can often be done more efficiently by computers. Attacks that aim to slow or stop targeted computers by blockading them require, in MVDA, many individuals, but could also be done by one individual utilizing programs. These are known as denial-of-service (DOS) attacks, because they seek to remove the target from the Internet, denying it service by overwhelming it with masses of requests for information. Such attacks have crippled major online sites such as ebay.com or yahoo.com. They are easily launched if small groups or even individuals use programs such as Stacheldracht. Oxblood Ruffin, foreign minister for the hacktivist group Cult of the Dead Cow, makes the following graphic comparison: 'The only difference between a program like Stacheldraht (a DOS application written by The Mixter) and the . . . Electrohippies is the difference between blowing some-thing up and being pecked to death by a duck.'[6]

The duck is preferable to the bomb for political, not technical, reasons. MVDA hacktivists seek to engage people, not just stop a targeted site. A mass of people is key, because then the protest is not about one person's technical abilities, but about the choice of many people to protest. This provides the same legitimation for a protest as thousands of people in the street might. It makes the protest a popular protest. The second political aim is to enrol people, to draw them into discussion, reflection and action. Many hacktivists call for debate prior to and after an action, using the communication resources of the Internet. This builds a movement offering many people who might be unable to attend a demonstration, for whatever reason, the chance to participate. It also allows a moment of commitment, perhaps a small one, in which people must decide whether they will or will not participate. A mass event needs the masses. Hacktivists producing denial-of-service actions choose a technically inefficient means to serve politically efficient ends.

However, a problem with the analogy to mass street protest is that when protesters block a street, it is impossible to miss the message and impossible for protesters to miss each other and the feeling of solidarity in the street, while in cyberspace, packets of information flowing across the Net are simply packets of information. Spikes of activity may be recorded on a targeted site, and the site's utility may be impaired by being slowed, but it is unclear whether the meaning of this action will be apparent to those on the receiving end. There are no passers-by in cyberspace. Whereas a street demonstration will reach whoever else happens to be in the vicinity – protesters and passers-by – and whoever watches media reporting, no such chance encounters will occur in cyberspace. Nor might solidarity really be built, as each protester will not know how many others are participating at the same time. Of course, all those who participate have some idea of what they are doing and why, but whether the protest registers more widely is unclear.

Virtual is the second component of MVDA, replacing non-violent when comparing MVDA and NVDA. This transition from violent to virtual needs explanation. The most often used means of explaining what is meant by virtual is to ask, 'When you are on the telephone, where does the conversation take place?' In your living room? But then your partner in communication is not there. In their room? But now you are absent. In the wires? But now both of your bodies are absent, yet still the communication occurs. Virtual communication is like this; it occurs in the wires. Such a place makes the notion of physical violence redundant, but violence may lurk within the virtual in two ways. First, many real-world institutions are affected by cyberspace. Computer networks control all sorts of real-world facilities, from dams and air-traffic control systems to financial institutions. Hacktivists do not automatically escape the possibility of violence by being virtual. Second, violence is not always physical, and damage to emotions and selves can occur in virtual lands. There have been long discussions about various sorts of emotional violence that have been inflicted in cyberspace. As long as an assault has dimensions in addition to physical ones, cyberspace can be home to a virtual version. In both of these ways, violence does not disappear for hacktivists, but must be rethought as they transgress information codes. As we will see later, for example, some argue that the violence hacktivists choose by utilizing denial-of-service attacks constitutes censorship.

Direct action is the third component of MVDA. The discussion of direct actions in Chapter 3 is applicable to MVDA as well as NVDA. MVDA attempts to take something on directly and prevent it. The clearest example is the attempt to mirror street protests halting the WTO Seattle conference by halting information flows serving that conference. Here, similar direct actions were taken in real and virtual spaces. However, MVDA rarely functions so clearly as a direct action. It can be weak as a direct action, because in cyberspace objects are easily replicated. This means that whereas a sit-in on a street can be difficult to move or a protest camp against a road can occupy a key piece of ground, in cyberspace the targeted computers can move. This can be done more or less simply and more or less expensively, but it is far more easily done in cyberspace than in real space. For example, all sites on the Internet are assigned a unique number that identifies them. When a denial-of-service MVDA is launched, it attacks the unique numbers of the targeted sites. However, it is possible to simply change the numbers and dodge an attack. Problems associated with such shifts should not be underestimated, but they offer opportunities to avoid MVDA that are not available offline. For these reasons, online direct actions may have greater effects as symbolic protests than as direct actions.

MVDA consists of these forces of mass, virtual and direct action. Each force interacts with the others in ways that have created a new class of civil disobedience. These actions bear many of the hallmarks of classic non-violent direct actions yet are passed through the looking glass of virtuality and become something different as electronic civil disobedience. These are new political moments that did not exist before the crossover of hacking and activism!. However, this does not mean that many previously existing actions taken by hackers have either disappeared or are irrelevant to hacktivism. Far from it. Many hacks have been reinvented as hacktivist actions, and an alternate vision of hacktivist politics has emerged with them. The deep concern of hackers for free, secure flows of information forms the second arm of hacktivism.

The Digitally Correct Hacktivist

For a long time, hackers' politics were closely tied to virtual issues – encryption, privacy, access. It is in hacking that we find traditional hacker pursuits such as cracking, developing tools to aid cracking and defending rights to secure, private communication. While these have always been concerns for hackers, the advent of hacktivism has given these actions a new political edge. The hacker group that perhaps best embodies this change is Cult of the Dead Cow (CDC), begun in 1984. The time during which they have been involved in the hacking community and digital issues shows that their work began well before hacktivism, yet they have also embraced it. Two of their projects show how the traditions of hacking have been given a new life with the politicization offered by hacktivism: Peekabooty and Back Orifice.

Peekabooty is the result of a group initiated by CDC working under the banner of Hacktivismo. This group targets censorship of the Internet by legitimating itself on the basis of the United Nations Declaration of Human Rights. This declaration asserts freedom of expression for all, including the freedom to receive as well as offer views. The Hacktivism Declaration states:

Hacktivismo is a special operations group sponsored by the CULT OF THE DEAD COW (CDC). We view access to information as a basic human right. We are also interested in keeping the Internet free of state-sponsored censorship and corporate chicanery so all opinions can be heard.[7]

The centrality of free flows of information, both to and from everyone, is clear. The concern prompting Hacktivismo is that a number of nation-states are limiting their citizens' access to the Internet. China is the example most often used, but there are other states that have established national firewalls to block politically sensitive material (firewalls are filtering mechanisms that control access to and from the Internet). For example, whether you can access CNN or the BBC online from within China has varied depending on whether the Chinese firewall has been set to allow it. A concrete initiative to address such problems is Peekabooty.

It seems clear that Peekabooty will be a network that anyone can use across the Internet to both bypass national firewalls, thereby gaining access to all information available on the Net, and to anonymize both senders and receivers of data. It is described as a 'distributed collaborative privacy network. It allows the evasion of most forms of . . . filtering and makes Web page requests directly to a distributed server cloud that processes the requests and trans-serves content back to the requesting client'.[8] Someone who is behind a firewall will be able to make a request to a computer running Peekabooty that will then establish a virtual network to a number of other computers (it is claimed that it will be difficult to detect whether Peekabooty is running on a network or not, but it may be possible to watch for Peekabooty, which will obviously undermine its utility). These 'other computers' form the 'server cloud', which simply means a number of other computers that transfer requests from the originating computer. Instead of requesting a known Internet site, whose address is blocked by the firewall, the request will be made to a Peekabooty-running computer that is not blocked by a firewall. This Peekabooty-running computer will then connect to the Peekabooty network. One of the computers connected to the network will access the requested material and pass it back through the server cloud to the original requesting computer. There will be no direct connection between requesting and responding computer, and each jump in between will ensure anonymity. These links through the server cloud will also shift dynamically – that is, they will change constantly. This means that a censoring government will have to constantly close down many Peekabooty-running computers to close the Peekabooty network down. Which ultimately means that as long as enough computers participate, closing Peekabooty will be difficult, if not impossible.

Should this network prove successful, it will provide a powerful antidote to national censorship. As Hacktivismo participants recognize, there is no guarantee that governments will not utilize powerful resources to prevent Peekabooty. For example, if a Peekabooty-running computer can be identified, then someone accessing that computer could be traced. Nevertheless, there is, to these hacktivists, a powerful incentive to try, as well as (it currently appears) the technical expertise to succeed.

Peekabooty attempts to prevent the erection of national borders in cyberspace. The focus on ensuring freedom of access to the Internet's huge store of information is also a focus on informational politics. In this sense, it differs from MVDA, which itself attempts to participate in an activist! campaign. The digitally correct hacktivist directly builds a particular informational politics; s/he is not building tools that serve other campaigns. This is similar to the distinction between pleasure-politics and pleasure and politics. MVDA-based actions are always for a cause, whereas digitally correct hacktivism is its own cause.

A second useful example is CDC's tool, Back Orifice. Back Orifice is a software program that allows anyone who uses a computer network based on Microsoft software to, among other things, secretly gain access to any other computer on the network. Back Orifice has a graphic user interface (GUI – that is, a point-and-click, mouse-based means of using programs) that makes it relatively easy to use. Installing Back Orifice means that the user will be able to look at the files on another computer, watch and record whatever someone is typing as they type and copy any files. All unprotected computers will be open to such intrusion. CDC have released a number of versions of Back Orifice and have made it open source, which means that the software code is available to anyone to alter and examine. In August 2001, Back Orifice was being downloaded from one site, it claimed, at an average of around a thousand times a day. By 2001, Back Orifice had developed to the extent that it was being presented as an alternative, free tool for network administrators to manage their Microsoft-based network.

The guide to Back Orifice (FAQ) explains: 'It was written with a twofold purpose: To enhance the Windows operating system's remote administration capability and to point out that Windows was not designed with security in mind.'[9] CDC's political rationale is to make clear that

Windows systems were not created with the security of the user in mind. CDC stress this by pointing out that all the stealth and secrecy capabilities of Back Orifice are already present in the systems-manager software written and sold by Microsoft. The ability to covertly look over anyone's shoulder onto their hard drive was present before Back Orifice, and remains present. Systems administrators utilize software tools with the same capabilities provided by CDC, except that Microsoft's code cannot be independently checked because the company hides it to retain their proprietary rights. One of CDC's aims with Back Orifice was to dramatize this already absent privacy on Microsoft-based networks, which their tool effectively does. Back Orifice 2000 was launched at the DefCon hacker conference as a moment of hacktivism and as part of a call to participate in changing the world.

As with Peekabooty, Back Orifice is a tool focused on the second key arena of hacktivism: ensuring privacy and security online with full access to information. Hacktivismo, as developed by CDC and others, sees little separation between these two issues and for good reason. Providing full access to the Internet in countries that seek to restrict it may be rendered meaningless if people and the sites they visit can be traced. The announcement of Hacktivismo includes this example: 'In August, 1998, eighteen year old Turk Emre Ersoz was found guilty of 'insulting the national police' in an Internet forum after participating in a demonstration that was violently suppressed by the police. His ISP provided the authorities with his address.'[10] Freedom to express your own views and receive all the information available on the Internet can be impaired both by restricting access and by refusing privacy. These two intertwined aims serve a virtual politics that is not restricted to the Internet, but is most at home there. The ability to access and offer information forms the central political principle of this arm of hacktivism.

Information, Irrelevance and Other Interests

Before concluding this chapter, it is important to note that hacktivism, like all the themes of activism!, can fail to develop the politics to which it claims to be committed. Unsurprisingly, MVDA hacktivists and digitally correct hacktivists are prone to different failures. Some of these difficulties have already been mentioned, but it will be useful to draw them together here.

As we have seen, the analogy between MVDA and street protest is ambiguous. While it is true that MVDA's allow many to participate who cannot physically be at a demonstration, at the same time those participating virtually do not take on the risk of the crowd or feel its solidarity. MVDA can perhaps be seen as an easy option. As Oxblood Ruffin said in criticism of an ehippies' MVDA, 'I know from personal experience that there is a difference between street and on-line protest. I have been chased down the street by a baton-wielding police officer on horseback. Believe me, it takes a lot less courage to sit in front of a computer.'[11] Not only might online protests fail to enrol and enthuse participants in the way street protests can; they may also allow those who might have participated to avoid confrontation. MVDA undoubtedly has potential, but it also has pitfalls.

Similarly, digitally correct hacktivism may create tools such as Back Orifice or Peekabooty, but there are also problems. This type of hacktivism aims to provide tools to ensure free flows of secure information; it makes – on a point of principle – little judgement concerning the nature of information sent in these free flows. The Hacktivismo FAQ exhibits this difficulty:

Q: Do you think all information should be accessible?
A: No. That's why we talk about 'lawfully published' information in the Hacktivismo Declaration. Essentially that cuts out things like legitimate government secrets, kiddie porn, matters of

personal privacy, and other accepted restrictions. But even the term 'lawfully published' is full of landmines. Lawful to whom? What is lawful in the United States can get you a bullet in the head in China. At the end of the day we recognize that some information needs to be controlled. But that control falls far short of censoring material that is critical of governments, intellectual and artistic opinion, information relating to women's issues or sexual preference, and religious opinions. That's another way of saying that most information wants to be free; the rest needs a little privacy, even non-existence in the case of things like kiddie porn. Everyone will have to sort the parameters of this one out for themselves.[12]

In this passage, 'lawfully published' information is sanctioned by hacktivism, but immediately this is subject to a critique that asks who defines what is lawful. There is a deep difficulty here between a principle of enabling flows of information and judging some types of information as wrong. The right to free flows of information can only, barely, take a stand against some of the most extreme forms of human exploitation. Digitally correct hacktivism may be a conduit for all sorts of politics, activisms of the past, present and future.

Codes of Information, Coding Transgression

Hacktivism has two currents that intertwine and separate. They also contradict each other. The current that places a premium on free flows of information sometimes sees little sense in the current that generates mass forms of online protest. This can be seen clearly in arguments around denial-of-service attacks. As already noted, denial of service is the restraint of information, the jamming and prevention of someone contributing to or receiving information, by preventing their website or Internet connections from working. CDC's response to the ehippies justification of their distributed denial-of-service actions criticized the ehippies denial of free flows of information:

> Denial of Service, is Denial of Service, is Denial of Service, period … Denial of Service attacks are a violation of the First Amendment, and of the freedoms of expression and assembly. No rationale, even in the service of the highest ideals, makes them anything than what they are – illegal, unethical, and uncivil. One does not make a better point in a public forum by shouting down one's opponent.[13]

It would be too strong to see such a divergence as some sort of split; hacktivism is not organized enough for such things as splits to appear. But it reflects the fact that two underlying politics of hacktivism may both contradict each other and transgress the information codes of 21st-century societies.

There are other types of hacktivist actions that circulate through and around these two major currents. Culture jamming finds a ready home on the Internet with hacktivists both propagating jams and cracking websites to recreate them jammed. On different occasions, the American Central Intelligence Agency's website has been renamed the Central Stupidity Agency, and political parties have found satirical cartoons inserted on their sites. On different political terrain, cracktivists break into networks to protest. After India tested nuclear weapons, a hacker gained entry to Indian government networks and threatened to trash them if the country persisted. These types of actions continue in and around hacktivism, but if we are seeking to grasp the innovations within activism! that hacktivism brings, then the two currents we have examined closely are key.

Hacktivists developing MVDA are fully immersed in the particular political ethics they support. The ehippies actions have supported the anti-globalization movement, EDT has plunged itself into Zapatista politics, and Netstrike has helped to fight judicial murder in the US. In these circumstances, the information flows are bent and twisted to invent new forms of mass protest that are no longer dependent on the co-presence of many tangible bodies. Here, hacktivism transgresses information codes to reproduce them as protest.

Hacktivists focusing on the importance of free flows of information are developing a politics in itself. In political terms, Peekabooty and Back Orifice are about nothing other than the virtual politics of secure access to information. The tools serve the ethics in ways that make them almost inextricably the same. Peekabooty, if it works, will embody in its very nature a commitment to the transgressive power of information on the Internet. Here, hacktivists are not so much bending, twisting and reshaping information flows as creating alternative infrastructures to enable new types of flow. Here, hacktivism transgresses information codes to recreate them as a politics of information.

Hacktivists of all types play in the information codes that form the infrastructures of 21st-century socio-economies. They transgress the flows of information both to create new forms of protest and to generate a new, activist politics of information. The geeks have emerged in politics. Activism! has hacktivisms within it.

CHAPTER SEVEN

Ethics, Activism, Futures

To plant the tree of tomorrow, that is what we want . . . The tree
of tomorrow is a space where everyone is, where the other knows
and respects the other others, and where the false light loses its
last battle.
Subcomandante Marcos[1]

The Meaning of Activism!

All sorts of movements, events, protests and people have marched through
these pages. Activists have written, struggled, fought, failed and won. The
protesters we have followed derive their activism from a leap in the dark,
from the unknowable; they transgress the present in the name of the
future. These activists are creating new ethical figures for society. These
new figures appear in direct actions that contradict accepted codes of political behaviour, in disorganized co-ordinations that reject hierarchy and
leadership, in collective pleasures that undermine authorized definitions of
what it is to be a person, in acts of semiotic terrorism that target cultural

137

norms of desire and needs, and in virtual actions in the informational structures of world socio-economies. But is the 'they', is activism!, something more than attacks on these five different social codes? Is it more than transgressions of political codes for creating social change, of organizational codes for hierarchial co-ordination, of regulatory codes for controlling selfhood, of cultural codes for defining desires and needs, and of informational codes for controlling knowledge? To fully grasp the meaning of activism!, we have to look for what activists might all, in their different, often contradictory, ways, be fighting for.

In deriving their ethics from the future, activists both rely on the unknown and begin to generate the known. There is constant pressure within activism! as it continues to be seduced by what it cannot quite articulate. This pressure is often made plain when activists are asked what their concrete plans for the future are. How will a society look after activism! succeeds? It is common for green activists to be asked how huge, complex, global cities like New York or Tokyo will work if the future is locally managed self-sustaining communities. It is common for feminists to be mocked for trying to undermine 'human nature' and to be asked to describe the details of a non-sexist society. It is common for activists of all sorts to be attacked by the bureaucrats of the present who demand to know, right now, what activism! wants. All of these demands register the unease activists can cause. They seek to reclaim activism! to the present and the past. However, such demands also implicitly recognize the tension within activism! between what is being created and the future that inspires it. It is, then, a misunderstanding to demand such blueprints from activists. To do so demands a turn from the new and the future to the known. Of course, this does not rule out asking activist!s what they want; it only rules out expecting detailed plans in return.

Accepting that it is a misunderstanding to demand that activist!s produce a detailed social programme, a blueprint for their desires, nonetheless leaves us with something to say about activism!'s vision of the better society. A number of guiding principles can be discerned, even now, resulting from this tension between present social change and future ethics. We can examine these principles to gain a sense of what activism! offers beyond the struggles of each movement. This will not offer us the social programmes demanded by present-day bureaucrats; it will be vaguer and more profound. It will mean shifting to an abstract discussion, because these principles are positioned both between and within movements.

The general principles of activism! cannot be found in just one movement, though they occur in all movements, but must be drawn from spaces between movements. While the argument so far has drawn ideas and events, abstract and concrete, together, we must now shift into a discussion of principle and ethics based on particular examples. For the first time, activism! will be seen to exist as an ethic. Another reason for shifting to an abstract discussion is that it will free us somewhat from the constraints of past and present embedded in the lived world. Abstractions can be rightly criticized for being detached from the 'real world', but that becomes a strength when looking to a future one.

In addition to looking at the the ethics of activism!, it is important to explore the consequences of these general principles in two directions. First, what is the relationship between activism! and democracy? Democracy and its institutions are necessarily engaged with a broader politics than that of any individual movement. It is important to see activism! in relation to such broader social organizations and ideas. Second, it is essential to reflect on the failures, potential and real, of activism!. Throughout this book, a component of activism! has been outlined to make sure that activism! is given a chance to be seen; it has then been critically examined. This method both undercuts a simple celebration of activism! and completes its story.

The story of activism! can be completed by reviewing three subjects: ethics, democracy and failure.

Ethics: Difference and Other

Activism!, as we have seen, is made up of many activist! movements. Each of these is itself differentiated and made up of many organizations, individuals, texts, events and so on. The first general principle of activism!, the one that is implicit within all previous discussion, is that of difference.

Particular campaigns or movements nearly always, at some point, have to react to the assertion of many inequalities and injustices, not necessarily the ones on which they have focused. For example, a pivotal moment within feminism occurred in the early 1980s, when issues were forcefully raised about who the 'woman' was who was being liberated. What was her colour, sexuality, religion, class or nationality? Another example is the anti-globalization movement, which is both inspired by demands (like Subcomandante Marcos's, for instance) to engage with all necessary liberations and which constantly has to negotiate between different understandings and definitions of liberation. One of the key early events in the formation of the anti-globalization movement was the 18 June (J18) global day of protest, which called for the targeting of financial centres. Here are some of the groups and protests planned for that day: North Sumatra Peasant Union, Chikoko (which organizes resistance to the oil industry in Nigeria), a mass 'laugh parade' in Cologne, Germany (to laugh at the G8 leaders), Reclaim the Streets London's closing of a financial futures exchange, a Chilean protest against the banning of street performance, and a feminist activist coalition in Albuquerque, New Mexico. In many of these instances, common forms of protest were planned, most often mass bicycle rides and/or street parties. Even given some common opponents (finance capital) and protest methods, the differences between participants in the J18 global street party were as striking as their similarities.

This mass of examples points to the centrality of different understandings of struggle. The question this difference creates is: 'What does it mean for difference to become a general ethical principle?' At first glance, the answer seems deceptively simple: Difference means the right of different politics to develop. Radical political activism! must be open and not closed. This relates to the historical point, made in Chapter 2, that while radical activism was for a time organized around a central political principle of capital versus labour, it no longer is. Activism! assumes many different movements with no single one drawing all of the threads together. When considered as an abstract principle, however, difference produces a surprising result: its opposite, indifference.

If there is a general principle that different political views must be allowed expression, then the underlying principle must relate to the means of doing so. One general principle of J18 was that all sorts of protests were both allowed and encouraged. This was so even if such protests were contradictory. For example, some protests had a nationalist bias, whereas many that opposed capitalism were internationalist, seeing nation-states as capital's handmaidens. Such contradictions could exist side by side because difference was invoked as a general principle. This means that when considering activism! overall, difference as a principle must be interpreted as the right of activist!s to create different movements. At an abstract level, this means that all political positions must be acceptable except for any position that rejects difference itself. Totalitarian or neo-fascist movements reject difference as a principle and so can be excluded or rejected, but no other politics can. When difference becomes a political principle, it produces a field of activism in which all activisms are acceptable as long as each, in its turn, accepts the rights of other activisms to be present. All politics other than the most extreme forms of authoritarianism can be considered equally as differences. Non-authoritarian, or legitimate, differences are mere differences.

We can see this in a non-activist example. Here is the definition of multiculturalism from a working group set up by and endorsed by the Australian government:

Australian multiculturalism is a term which recognises and cele-
brates Australia's cultural diversity. It accepts and respects the
right of all Australians to express and share their individual
cultural heritage within an overriding commitment to Australia
and the basic structures and values of Australian democracy.[2]

Asserting the rights of all Australians to be different means also asserting
the rights of Australians who have racist or anti-racist cultural beliefs. It
means asserting the cultural rights of some who have social practices
abhorrent to others. This assertion of difference, as if difference itself is
something Australian, is from a country that has over the previous ten
years seen the rise and fall of a populist far-right movement, the One
Nation Party, and a failing national government that rescued its election
prospects by refusing to let asylum seekers touch down on its land. It is a
nation in which a central issue of cultural diversity is that of its indigenous
peoples, whose claim for land rights necessarily asserts a different relationship to the nation than other Australians can possibly have. For
Aboriginal peoples to have rights to land, as we have seen, they had to have
their existence prior to European settlement recognized. This means that
for the powerful oppressions and near-genocide against Aboriginal peoples
to be ameliorated, a key factor will be recognizing that Aboriginal peoples
have a claim to be different Australians than all other Australians. But the
multicultural statement does not allow this; all Australians are equally
different. We see here a deradicalization of difference and the production
of difference as 'mere differences'. We see the seemingly anti-racist and
anti-xenophobic stance of multiculturalism turned into a setting in which
racist 'differences' are acceptable, but indigenous 'differences' are not.
Difference becomes indifferent, unable to distinguish between politics
except for opposing totalitarianism.

Difference, paradoxically, results in an undifferentiated politics. It is a
politics that has an inside and an outside, with a boundary drawn by total-

itarianism's refusal of the rights of difference. When difference as multi-plicity becomes the foundation of a politics, it is as if all politics is conducted in the difference between splinters of essentially like-minded activists. Difference no longer makes a difference.

Ethics: Other and Oppression

Despite difference's inherent deradicalization, it remains central to activism!. The multiplicity of politics within activism! remains founda-tional for the historical and ethical reasons already discussed. Instead of rejecting difference, we need to explore the second pillar of activism!'s ethics: oppression and otherness.

Oppression and Otherness is a name for the way many activism!s conceive themselves as opposing social relations in which one community is exploited by at least one other community. These exploitations may occur in many ways; labour, culture, time, money and self-determination may all be extracted from one community by one or more communities. For example, nearly all surveys of patterns of housework taken in the Northern, or overdeveloped, countries show that women do the majority of such work, even when work outside the home is done equally by men and women. It does not seem to matter greatly how much work, usually paid, is done by men or women outside the home when labour inside the home is examined. This means that the daily labour of maintaining a clean, safe home is undertaken by women, but enjoyed by men and women. Men here extract free domestic labour from women. Men exploit women. This is not a new or unusual claim; it has been heard from the feminist move-ment for years and confirmed by survey after survey. We could pursue this example to explore further inequalities or exploitations; men earn more for doing the same work, women work less and in less secure jobs, and so on. This is just one example of the general point that exploitation occurs when one group of people, in this example men, gain some advantage over another group, here women, in a way that simultaneously impoverishes the exploited community. It is not just that men gain a clean home without working for it, but that women also lose the time and effort needed to create that home, and men could not benefit without women losing.

A problem with oppression is that it is often interpreted economically. Not only is the concept of exploitation a technical term within Marxist theory, but there is a tendency to collapse oppression back into monetary terms. But oppression occurs in many different ways. The inability of women to walk safely at night in the street, the inability of indigenous communities to maintain their essential cultural relations to land, the extraction of 'normality' for heterosexuals through the imposition of deviance on gays, lesbians, bisexuals and transsexuals – all these and more point to a concept of oppression that has to include, but reach beyond, socio-economic understandings. That is why the philosophical concept of Self and Other is useful, though extracted from its complex background and simplified; it abstracts discussion from socio-economic relations and refuses, through its terminology, the reduction of all social relations to money. Others are the exploited, created in the formation of a Self. Men create themselves as men, they define their Selves and what it means to be a man, by establishing and maintaining social relations that create women as the Other. Others are the oppressed, and the more abstract language helps extract such definitions from the economic realm and make it clear there is far more at stake than the pay packet, however important that is.

Selves and Others can be joined in antagonism and exploitation. Activism! pitches itself, in all its various guises, on the ground of difference and against social exploitations. Activism! confronts exploitations: feminism attacking the exploitation of women Others by male Selves; anti-racism confronting relations between White Selves dominating Black Others; environmentalism defying a split between exploitation of ecology Selves and care for ecology Others; and many more. The failures of difference, that it falls away into mere differences, is made good by this focus on the ways in which communities or collectives damage each other to take advantage of each other. To prevent difference from evacuating the politics of liberation into nothing but mere difference, activism! recognizes the perversion of collective Self/Other relations. It recognizes ruthless and brutal exploitations of one or more collective peoples by one or more other collectives. Difference ensures that activism! includes within it struggles against many forms of exploitation and refuses the sometimes-invoked game of deciding which exploitation is the key one. There does not have to be one Self and one Other; combinations of Selves and Others can be expected. The search for the most basic form of oppression, from which all others derive, is refused within activism!. There is no hierarchy of oppression; there is no need for one people's being attacked and damaged on a daily, social basis by another people to compete with any other repressed group. Instead, all such relations must be exposed and fought.

We should expect oppressive relations to involve several interlocking relationships of exploitation. In this way, we might understand how a working class in a colony can be positioned simultaneously as Other by the colonial ruling class and as Self, or part of the imperial nation, in regard to colonized Others. Similarly, men can be positioned as part of a working-class Other, a patriarchal Self and either a racialized Self or Other. What appears to be a binary relation of Self and Other is, instead, a fully differentiated and multiple set of social relations.

This multiplicity partly explains why 'power' has become a key term within activism! and social thought generally. Social antagonisms have often been defined through their substantial social relations: for example, workers exploited by bosses through control of working conditions and the products of the workplace would have been called capitalism; men controlling women through sexual double-standards and subordination to domesticity would have been called patriarchy; and so on. To draw together all of these many different struggles, a term as insubstantial, yet evocative, as 'power' has been needed. Hall expressed this importance of this term:

> I know power is a very abstract term – patriarchal power is very different from governmental power and very different from economic power – but 'power' is used as the way of naming the enemy . . . 'power' is used as a way of naming, generally, exclusion from power, exclusion from the capacity to have access to power which could make a change or make a difference.[3]

'Power' is the term that fills the gap, which in one word allows reference to all of the diverse exploitations and oppressions of this world without implying that they are the same exploitations and oppressions. Activism! fights Power, activist!s want to dissolve Power; but to understand what this means, we have to understand that there are many relations of power, each of which refers to the exploitation of Others by Selves. We have reached the fundamental principles of activism!'s vision of the better world, or as much of them as I can discern being brought from the future to inform popular protest: difference *and* oppression.

What is Democracy?

Having extracted two ethical principles from the confused mass of activism!, we can stay at a general level to explore what they mean. It is particularly important to see how such principles might inform key political institutions, of which democracy is perhaps the most important. Activism! develops a commitment to democracy to ensure that difference can be expressed. If social life is closed and there are no ways for social solidarities and antagonisms to be recognized and dis/organized, then relations of Selves and Others will fail to generate collective actions.

Democracy within activism! results from the necessity of creating social solidarities and fighting oppressions. Some social space must be open to the dis/organization of movements, otherwise there is no way for either solidarity or antagonism to be recognized and struggled over.

It would, however, be a mistake to think that activism! is committed to many current forms of democracy, which offer only the disillusioning prospect of voting every four or so years to give power to one of two similar political groups. This is all the more true when most such systems offer a choice between groups who often agree on promoting some social antagonisms. Across the overdeveloped world, there is hardly any government that has been willing to reject the neo-liberal vision of globalization that has produced, in reaction to its inequities, such heroes of activism! as the Zapatistas and many peasant movements. Democracies that offer little choice both disillusion and disempower. For democracy to be a meaningful political commitment, as it must be, it must itself be reconceived. A commitment to democracy will hardly seem radical, unless democracy is radicalized.[4] Two paths of radicalization are needed: representation and articulation. These can be seen in the Zapatista articulation of the need for a new civil society, a new social space in which oppressions can be articulated and resistance created.

In 2001, the Zapatistas, the indigenous and peasant movement in southern Mexico, set out on a tour of the country. This was remarkable, as the Zapatistas had been in armed opposition for seven years. Even more remarkably, they travelled around most of Mexico stopping off and speaking in many communities, finally arriving in the capital, Mexico City. Their rally there drew hundreds of thousands of people, and, soon after, Zapatista representatives spoke to the Mexican Congress. While all of this is extraordinary enough, what is interesting when considering democracy and activism! is how a guerrilla movement, addressing a supposedly democratic body, understood its relations to leadership and representation. Consider these words spoken by Comandante Esther:

Some might have thought that this tribune would be occupied by
... Marcos, and that it would be he who would be giving this main
message of the Zapatistas. You can now see that it is not so.
Subcomandante Insurgente Marcos is that, a Subcomandante. We
are the Comandantes, those who command jointly, the ones who
govern our peoples, obeying.[5]

First, Esther noted that many saw the charismatic Marcos as the leader of
the Zapatistas, but this was not so. Instead, there were Comandantes who
spoke and who believed that they could only lead by obeying. These words
echoed earlier proclamations by the Zapatistas. Most notably, in the
Fourth Declaration of the Lacandon Jungle, they called for a new democra-
tizing and grass-roots movement throughout Mexico, for a 'political force
which can organize the demands and proposals of those citizens and is
willing to give direction through obedience'.[6] This call for a different form
of social organization was further enunciated as a 'new radical democratic
imaginary for Mexico'[7] and, by implication, a new democratic imagination
for the world. Though a movement with a military arm and all of the hierarchical necessities that this entails, the Zapatistas see the opening up of a
new form of democracy as essential. This can only be done by radicalizing
the existing forms of representation and ways of defining interests that
need representation. These two sides form the essential intervention into
democracy that activism! brings.

First, the representation of different views and interests through
formal democratic systems needs to be radicalized. This involves the prolif-
eration of democratic arenas and mechanisms. Local, regional, national
and international democratic organizations need to be generated so that
those oppressed at all of these levels can find appropriate places in which
they can be represented. The mechanisms by which representation is
produced also need to proliferate. There needs to be multiplicity not only
in the types of places in which representatives meet and decide, but also in

the different forms by which representations can be produced. From the direct democracy of referenda to ensuring that decisions are taken by representatives openly and accountably, all means of making democratic decisions need to be explored.

Second, all around the institutions of a radicalized representative democracy, new spaces are needed in which democratization can proceed. Ways are needed through which people can find others who are Other like them. Places are needed in which those who are repressed can begin to oppose repression. Activism! must fight not only for a democracy appropriate to the powerless, but for those hard-to-define spaces in which the powerless can come to understand what their liberation might be. Access to and the radicalization of media are necessary for a radical democracy.

This is merely a general outline, yet it establishes something essential in activism!. It shows how the general ethical principles of activism! can result in demands for change not only at the level of each movement but also more generally. Radical democracy, the transgression of current systems of democratic representation and of current forms of civil society, is an activist! aspiration.

Activism! and its Potential

This commitment to radicalized democracy is a glimpse of a possible future offered by activism!'s ethics, but there are others that may be less attractive. We have focused so far in this chapter on excavating the importance of difference and oppression to activism! at a general level. This so far positions activism! as an almost saintly presence, offering a vision for a better world. This is partly true, yet we also need to be critical and to see where less attractive eventualities lie within activism!. One place to start is with terrorism.

A consequence of the commitment to difference and its expression in radicalized democracy should be that activism!, at its heart, rejects terrorism. In a world likely to be riven for some time to come by the most powerful nations' announcement of war in response to horrific terrorist acts, this might seem an obvious position to adopt. But it is worth noting that it develops from core principles of activism!. Without venturing too far into the difficult conceptual terrain of defining terrorism, we can take it to be violence for political ends designed both to have far-reaching psychological effects and to achieve its ends by imposing its views.[8] Such a position should be deeply antithetical to the ethics so far outlined in this chapter, as the commitment to radical democracy shows.

But we already saw when discussing direct action how violence may become a tactical issue within activism!. Terror within activism! is undoubtedly a rare occurrence, but we cannot ignore the animal liberationists to whom terror is a legitimate tactic. We see a tension here within activism!. Terrorism is a negation of difference; it seeks the elimination of opposition through psychological panic, and activism!'s ethics are opposed to such a closure of political debate. However, activism!'s commitment to direct action can lead to gradual slippage from non-violence to violence against property and against people. While it would be astonishing to term activism! terrorist and absurd to link it to terrorist acts such as that of 11 September, we must also be aware of pressures within activism! which lead elsewhere than a 'paradise' of difference and liberation.

We have touched on a number of other problems that emerge from within activism!, and it is important to draw them together. Dis/organization gone wrong offers the possibility of endless meetings, no one of which has the power to finalize decisions. The bad, stale, old jokes about activists preferring meetings to social change here return to haunt. When we see the Zapatistas wishing to reconceive democracy and civil society partially in line with dis/organizational principles, we can be thrilled, but we must also be aware of the potential difficulties. Writing the failed forms of dis/organization across society can lead to hierarchies that are not only hidden, but are held to be, on principle, non-existent. It can lead to an inability to come to decisions and to close debates until time makes them absolutely essential, at which point they will be made suddenly and with little regard to representation.

Pleasure-politics offers the possibility of a self-interested, self-righteous definition of social change. The necessary solipsism of such politics opens the way to mysticism and disengagement from society. The shift within the hippie movement to communes that rejected society and completely separated themselves from it is one example. Self-regarding and self-defined communities can abandon their engagements with culture and self that made them transgressive, instead seeking liberation in a god, a pill or a shaman.

Culture jamming is subject to a recuperation in which oppressors benefit from what was thought to be transgressive. At its worst, we might see culture jamming as simply extending the Empire of Signs, as pushing branding techniques ever further into our subconscious understandings of desire. Instead of opposing advertisers' manipulation of our needs, perhaps, at its worst, culture jamming is a laboratory of techniques available to the professionals of branding. Perhaps culture jamming undermines semiotic transgression by undermining our faith that symbolic transgressions can be part of attacking oppression and not be part of the manipulation of our symbolic codes.

Finally, hacktivism can be caught between offering technical tools for other struggles or drifting into an isolated information-based virtual politics. The dilemma of hacktivism may be either to serve politics, which hacktivists must learn to judge for themselves, or to serve themselves on the terrain of cyberspace. Perhaps hacktivism is either diverting struggle into the virtual realm, or for any politics the virtual realm is perfect.

Beyond these failures of activism! and also encompassing them are two temptations of activism! for activists. There are two ways of reconceiving activism!'s ethics that turn away from the future and begin to live in the present or even the past; there are inherent problems in activism! at a general level.

The first temptation is to focus on democracy and lose the radical edge of oppression, to focus on talking and enabling but not opposing. This results in a thin politics ultimately based on the notion that 'all differences are politically legitimate.' Such a conception is tempting; it leans heavily on social inclusion and offers concrete campaigns in many areas for improving democracy. Yet it is ultimately futile, as not all differences are equal or legitimate. There must be ways of understanding that the 'difference' of the ultra-rich is not a cultural or political difference that should be defended, but the result of bitter and ongoing exploitation. Similar problems can be seen when powerful Selves emerge to claim their difference: White, male, Western, heterosexual. A politics focused purely on processes of democracy cannot grasp at anything substantial. It becomes a politics of means without ends; it is multiculturalism in the hands of the state. Difference remains essential, and radical democracy integral, to activism!, yet they are not enough.

The second temptation is to make one oppression absolute and fundamental. For most of the twentieth century, this was the constant temptation of the left – the temptation to make class the founding form of exploitation from which all others flowed. This is a powerful temptation, still active, for example, in Hardt and Negri's astonishing call for a new communism based on a return to Marxist virtues. It is a temptation registered every time the anti-globalization movement of the early 21st century slips from opposing certain forms of globalization to homogenizing all struggles under the banner of anti-capitalism. Even if it seems that it is surely too late in the history of emancipatory struggles to give in again to this temptation, it remains an ever-present possibility. We might think that there are simply too many exploitations, each structured in its own way, to clutch at the belief that destroying one such relationship will somehow lead to the end of all Otherness, but it remains a temptation.

However positive and at times celebratory this account of activism! might seem – and I believe there is much to celebrate – there are also critical points to be made. There are activist! futures that look less bright, new dawns I hope never to see. Having laid these out and emphasized them – perhaps in some cases (particularly violence) over-emphasized them – we can conclude by looking again at activism! as a form of hope, as an aspiration drawn from the future.

Activism!

A potential lies within activism!, the possibility of a new ethical basis for society. This potential flickers, is sometimes clear and sometimes fades away. Throughout the various actions that contest social codes, these ethics take form and deform. The ethics of activism! exist in direct actions contesting society's construction: in dis/organizations prefiguring anti-hierarchical social co-ordination; in collective pleasures contesting subordination to the social factory; in cultural interventions against the language of corporate and state desire; and in hacktivism's interventions in electronic codes. Throughout these various actions, activism! produces ways of being and ethics. The nature of movements and their constant generation of collective identities, which themselves are constantly renegotiated between activist!s, means that the immanent ethics of activism! may never appear finished. Yet this does not prevent it achieving an articulation such as that I have given in this book. Activism!'s ethics of the future are both real and constantly developing.

Activism!'s ethics of the future offer us a vision of a movement-based society in which the representation and generation of different ways of life is constantly, radically open. This is not a vision in which everyone becomes an activist!. Perhaps put more accurately, this is a vision that demands that we rethink what is meant by political activity. Solidarities and oppressions that gain collective expression become the central motors of social change and social definition. Being an activist! in such a society can mean many things and need not mean being someone who chains themselves to bulldozers, hacks websites or attends endless meetings. Instead, what it means to be an activist! is transformed as the work of achieving social solidarities and sustaining campaigns against exploitation become central to the building of a better society. Here, the politics of pleasure points the way forward most clearly. Within pleasure-politics, we see people not so much engaging in politics as accidentally, perhaps carelessly, finding that they have transgressed regulatory codes of personality and self. Having done this, they may become overtly politicized or not, yet a politics is nonetheless occurring. Just as transgression may be accidental, so anyone can find themselves beginning to recognize their potential for creating new social forms. Small actions are just as central to activism! as large ones.

The future is anything but assured. We are not examining laws of history here, but the ways in which people make their own societies, under all sorts of conditions and carrying all sorts of burdens. This making of society is a contradictory and conflict-ridden process. There is no guarantee that either politics of the past or present will not succeed or that the already powerful will not find ways to continue their domination. If anything, the latter may – terrifyingly – be the smart bet.

The fact that the future is always uncertain is its attraction. The temptations of activism! and its opponents – the past, the present and the powerful – make the future one we cannot predict with any certainty. We can, however, see a possible future. We can understand a different ethical basis for human societies. We can sometimes clearly and sometimes vaguely discern the structures of a different definition of a just way of living. This is based on the radical democratization of representing and generating social interests and on conflict with exploitation: solidarity and exploitation, care and neglect, difference and Self/Other. What activism!

offers is a broad, radical and revolutionary vision of what must be opposed in our existing world and what might be loved in a future one. Activism! perhaps finally justifies its exclamation.

References

One: Societies in Pieces, Movements in Action

1 D. Wall, *Earth First! and the Anti-Roads Movement* (London, 1999), p. 40.
2 Margery Lewis, cited in S. Roseneil, *Disarming Patriarchy* (Buckingham, 1995), p. 36.
3 M. Lee, *Earth First! Environmental Apocalypse* (New York, 1995), p. 57.
4 V. Woolf, cited in M. Bradbury and J. McFarlane, eds, *Modernism* (Harmondsworth, 1976), p. 33.
5 M. Young and P. Willmott, *Family and Kinship in East London* (London, 1957), p. 27.
6 See M. Castells, *The Power of Identity: The Information Age, Volume II* (Oxford, 1997), Chap. Four, for one summary.

Two: Transgression: Reforming, Reactionary and Visionary

1 J. Borger, 'Thousands of Mothers Tell Gun Lobby: Enough Is Enough',

Guardian Newspaper/GuardianUnlimited, 15 May 2000, available at
www.guardianunlimited.co.uk/archive

2 Available at http://www.actlab.utexas.edu/~zapatistas/faqs.html

3 I must stress that I mean that, in formal terms, the corruption of Mexico's
government and its association with strongly anti-indigenous rights-
organizations means that, in fact, some of the victories of *Zapatismo* have
required shifts within the country's governmental systems.

4 Marcos, *Our Word is Our Weapon: Selected Writings – Subcomandante Marcos*,
ed. Juana Ponce de León (London, 2001), p. 280.

5 W. Peirce, 'The New World Order, "Free" Trade, and the Deindustrialization of
America', *National Vanguard* (March 1995), available at
http://www.natvan.com/national-vanguard/assorted/newworldorder.html

6 'Under Fire, Pentagon Says German Training Center NOT a Base', *CNN*,
available at www.cnn.com/US/9605/03/greman.airbase/index.html

7 NamVeto49, 'Ready to be Disarmed?', *Taking Aim*, 6/10 (2000), available at
http://www.militiaofmontana.com/takeaim.htm

8 K. Maue, 'What Is the Militia?', available at
http://www.militiaofmontana.com/whomom.htm

9 'From Recruit to Renegade: Timothy McVeigh', *ABCNews*, available at
http://more.abcnews.go.com/sections/us/oklahoma/mcveigh.html

Three: Action and Dis/Organization

1 P. Ackerman and J. Duvall, *A Force More Powerful: A Century of Non-violent
Conflict* (New York, 2000), pp. 61–112.

2 B. Doherty, 'Manufactured Vulnerability: Protest Camp Tactics', in B. Seel, M.
Paterson and B. Doherty, eds, *Direct Action in British Environmentalism*
(London, 2000), pp. 62–78.

3 Anon A, 'Street Politics 2000', available at http://www.gn.apc.org/rts/street-
politics.htm

4 Anon B, 'On the Attack in Prague!: Against the IMF and the World Bank', *Do
or Die*, 9 (2000), pp. 1–8, p. 7.

5 Anon C (2000), 'Here Comes the Barmy Army!: Pink and Silver on the Warpath', *Do or Die*, 9 (2000), pp. 12–14, pp. 13–14.

6 Cited on Justice Department website available at http://www.animalliberation.net/library/facts/jd.html

7 Anon D (2000), 'On Dis/organisation: A Statement from Reclaim the Streets (RTS) London', available at http://www.gn.apc.org/rts/disorg.htm

8 Available at http://www.actupny.org/

9 'Here Comes the Barmy Army!', pp. 12–13.

10 Available at http://www.sei.ukshells.co.uk/.

11 S. Wright, 'Changing the World (One Bridge at a Time?): Ya Basta! after Prague; Interview with Hobo', available at http://www.geocities.com/swervedc/yabasta.html

12 Wright, 'Changing the World...'.

Four: Pleasure as a State Crime

1 S. Reynolds, *Energy Flash: A Journey through Rave Music and Dance Culture* (London, 1998), p. xv.

2 Andy, *Rave: The Spiritual Dimension* (Liphook, 1994), p. 25.

3 For more detailed accounts, see S. Garratt, *Adventures in Wonderland: A Decade in Club Culture* (London, 1998); Reynolds, *Energy Flash*.

4 H. Rietveld, 'Living the Dream', in, S. Redhead, ed., *Rave Off: Politics and Deviance in Contemporary Youth Culture* (Aldershot, 1993), pp. 41–78, p. 63.

5 Andy, *Rave*, p. 4.

6 D. Hemment, 'House without a Home', paper given at the 'Shouts from the Street Conference on Popular Culture', Manchester, 1995, p. 5.

7 A. Melucci, *Challenging Codes: Collective Action in the Information Age* (Cambridge, 1996), p. 71.

8 Push and M. Scott, *The Book of E: All about Ecstasy* (London, 2000), p. 90.

9 *Ibid.*, p. 98.

10 M. A. Wright, 'The Great British Ecstasy Revolution', in G. McKay, ed., *DiY Culture: Party and Protest in Nineties Britain* (London, 1998), pp.

228–42, p. 235.

11 Wright, 'The Great British Ecstasy Revolution', p. 236.

12 Garratt, *Adventures in Wonderland*, p. 116.

13 Wright, 'The Great British Ecstasy Revolution', pp. 232–3.

14 R. Huq, 'The Right to Rave: Opposition to the Criminal Justice and Public Order Act 1994', in T. Jordan and A. Lent, eds, *Storming the Millennium: The New Politics of Change* (London, 1999), pp. 15–34, p. 28.

Five: Culture Jamming and Semiotic Terrorism

1 M. Dery, 'Culture Jamming: Hacking, Slashing and Sniping in the Empire of Signs', *Open Magazine Pamphlet Series: Pamphlet 25, 1993*, p. 5.

2 Available at http://www.adbusters.org/uncommercials/

3 J. Napier, 'Letter to Seth Maxwell 1998', available at http://www.billboardliberation.com/actions/turk.letter.html

4 And can be seen at http://www.billboardliberation.com/actions/turk.html

5 Napier, 'Letter to Seth Maxwell'.

6 Available at http://www.billboardliberation.com/

7 All available at http://www.adbusters.org/spoofads/

8 Available at http://www.adbusters.org/creativeresistance/jamgallery/street/

9 Dery, 'Culture Jamming', pp. 5–6.

10 Cited in R. Atkinson, *Crusade: The Untold Story of the Gulf War* (London, 1993), p. 161. Brackets added by Atkinson.

11 Available at http://www.rtmark.com.

12 Brian Holmes, cited in J. Crandall, *Drive: Technology, Mobility and Desire* (New York, 2002), pp. 222–3.

13 Available at http://www.nikesweatshop.net

14 Available at http://www.spacehijackers.co.uk/html/projects/boxfreshres.html

Six: Hacktivism: All Together in the Virtual

1 CAE (Critical Art Ensemble), *Electronic Civil Disobedience and Other Unpopular Ideas* (New York, 1996).

2 Electrohippies Collective (2000), 'Client-side Distributed Denial-of-Service: Valid Campaign Tactic or Terrorist Act?; Occasional Paper no. 1', available at http://www.gn.apc.org/pmhp/ehippies

3 Though it should be made clear that the two are technically different.

4 Electrohippies Collective (2001), 'The FTAA Action and May Day "Cyber-Hysteria" communiqué May 2001', available at http://www.gn.apc.org/pmhp/ehippies

5 Quoted from Netstrike website then being mirrored at http://www.contrast.org/netstrike/howto/istruzioni_en.html At the time of writing, the main site, www.netstrike.it, had been blocked by Italian magistrates.

6 O. Ruffin, 'Valid Campaign Tactic or Terrorist Act?: The Cult of the Dead Cow's Response to Client-side Distributed Denial-of-Service 2000', available at http://www.gn.apc.org/pmhp/ehippies

7 Cult of the Dead Cow, 'The Hacktivismo FAQ', available at http://www.cult-deadcow.com/cDc_files/HacktivismoFAQ.html

8 *Ibid.*; for demonstrations of Peekabooty, see TechTV reports available at http://www.techtv.com/print/story/0,23102,3337379,00.html

9 CDC (2001), 'Back Orifice 2000 FAQ', available at http://www.bo2k.source-forge.net/

10 CDC and Hacktivismo (2001), 'A Special Message of Hope', available at http://www.cultdeadcow.com/cDc_files/declaration.html

11 Ruffin, 'Valid Campaign Tactic'.

12 Cult of the Dead Cow, 'The Hacktivismo FAQ'.

13 Ruffin, 'Valid Campaign Tactic'.

Seven: Ethics, Activism, Futures

1 Marcos, *Our Word Is Our Weapon: Selected Writings – Subcomandante Marcos,* ed. Juana Ponce de León (London, 2001), p. 282.

2 Available at http://www.immi.gov.au/multicultural/nmac/summ-a.htm

3 Cited in T. Jordan and A. Lent, *Storming the Millennium: The New Politics of Change* (London, 1999), pp. 214-15.

4 The phrase 'radical democracy' has been explored in the work of E. Laclau and C. Mouffe, though not only by them. See C. Mouffe, *The Democratic Paradox* (London, 2000); E. Laclau and C. Mouffe, *Hegemony and Socialist Strategy,* 2nd edn (London, 2001).

5 Available at http://www.narconews.com/zcongress.html

6 Marcos, 'Fourth Declaration of the Lacandon Jungle 1996', available at http://flag.blackened.net/revolt/mexico/ezlnco.html, 1996.

7 *Ibid.*

8 D. Whittaker, *The Terrorism Reader* (London, 2001).

Acknowledgements

Thanks to all those who participated in all sorts of ways in what has now been a long involvement in (studying?) popular protest and radical politics. Particular thanks in more recent times, and whether they knew it or not, to all at Brainstorms, Jim Carey, Rachel Cottam, Ricardo Dominguez, Peter Hamilton, Brian Holmes, John Jordan, Chris Kelly, Adam Lent, George McKay, Paul Mobbs, Alex Plows, Jai Redman, Paul Taylor, Alain Touraine, Merl Storr and all those at Reaktion Books. Special thanks to Andrea Watts.

As ever, no thanks are adequate for Kate, Matilda and Joanna; the great adventure continues.

List of Illustrations